ANCIENT CIVILIZATIONS

Comparing and Contrasting Cultures

Written by
Sandy Sturmer

Published by World Teachers Press®
www.worldteacherspress.com

Order Number 2-5201
ISBN 978-1-58324-140-0

L M N O P 21 20 19 18 17

395 Main Street
Rowley, MA 01969
www.didax.com

Foreword

Ancient Civilizations is a book of reproducible worksheets for upper elementary and middle school students. The activities are designed to provide information and opportunities for the students to gain a comprehensive overview of ten of the world's ancient civilizations.

Each of the ten civilizations in the book comprises a set of activity pages in which the students focus on the customs, culture, lifestyles, inventions and historical data relating to each civilization.

Student activities include:

- *Researching, collating and categorizing information*
- *Comparing and contrasting lifestyles and cultures*
- *Constructing time lines*
- *Organizing, recording and interpreting data*
- *Mapping activities*
- *Collaborative and decision-making activities*
- *Appreciating cultural differences*
- *Creating and designing arts and crafts models*

The focus of this book is to create an awareness of the importance of the contributions made by each civilization, and to promote an appreciation of the influences each of these civilizations has had on the world as it is today.

Contents

Teacher's Notes

The activities included in this book develop the following skills and strategies.

- Plans an investigation by identifying and using information from more than one source, and makes inferences from the information collected in order to justify personal decisions.
- Understands that natural processes affect the natural and built features of places and these features have an influence on human activity and on people's views about which places need to be cared for.
- Understands that efficient use and management of resources increases the ability to satisfy needs and wants.
- Understands that the diverse groups to which people belong vary in their traditional and non-traditional aspects and that interaction with these groups influences the identity of individuals.
- Understands that people and events in a time period are linked through the impact each has on the other and that there are different perspectives on people and events of the past.

Resources
Students should be encouraged to use a variety of resources to complete their activities:

- *Encyclopedias* – Written and CD-Rom
- *Resource books and atlases*
- *Computer information retrieval systems* – Internet (Suggested Internet websites are provided for each civilization.)

Suggested Uses for this Book
- *Individual Student Activity* – Each set of activities may be completed individually by the students.
- *Group Activity* – Students may work in small groups of two to four and combine their answers to compile a group report.
- *Individual Workcards* – Activities may be transferred to card and laminated to be used as individual research activity cards.
- *Project or Homework Activity* – Activities may be used as a home-based project activity to be completed by the student independent of school.
- *Multicultural Stimulus Activity* – Activities could be used to stimulate a theme of multiculturalism and to compare and contrast ancient cultures and modern cultures.

Additional Material Provided
- *Quiz Sheet* (page 8) – The quiz questions may be used as a pre-test and/or as a review test to assess prior and present knowledge about the topics.

Ancient Civilizations – Quiz Sheet

Name: _____   Date: _____

Answer the following questions about the ancient civilizations of the world.

1. Which civilization built the Sphinx?
2. Montezuma II was one of the rulers of which civilization?
3. Which civilization used tattoos on their face as a form of decoration?
4. Which civilization has beliefs called "the Dreaming"?
5. The Olympic Games was first developed by which civilization?
6. Hiram Bingham discovered the remains of the "Lost City" called Machu Picchu, which was built by which civilization?
7. Who wore a toga?
8. Which civilization built Hadrian's Wall to keep out the Scots?
9. Which civilization lived in homes called tepees?
10. Who wore a chiton or a peplon?
11. Which civilization built their cities along the River Nile?
12. Which civilization enjoyed the dance called the haka?
13. Who traveled in longships?
14. The kimono was worn by the people of which civilization?
15. Who ate pancakes called tortillas?
16. Which civilization used a quipu as a method of calculation?
17. Which civilization had a ruler whose name was Atahuallpa?
18. Which civilization used a travois attached to a horse to pull their belongings?
19. Who invented the Julian calendar?
20. Which civilization was ruled by families called dynasties?
21. The Acropolis and the Parthenon were built by the people of which civilization?
22. Which civilization of people made baskets from pandanus palm fronds?
23. The pharaoh was the name of the ruler of which civilization?
24. Which civilization of people earned a reputation as raiders and traders?
25. Which civilization built their city on an island in the middle of Lake Texcoco?
26. Spiral designs were a feature of which civilization's artwork and carvings?
27. To which civilization did the tribe called the Comanche belong?
28. Who used the runic alphabet?
29. Paper was invented by which civilization?
30. Who used a woomera to throw a spear?

Score: /30

Quiz Sheet Answers

1. Egyptians		2. Aztecs	
3. Maori		4. Aboriginal Australians	
5. Greeks		6. Inca	
7. Romans		8. Romans	
9. American Indians		10. Greeks	
11. Egyptians		12. Maoris	
13. Vikings		14. Chinese	
15. Aztecs		16. Inca	
17. Inca		18. American Indians	
19. Romans		20. Chinese	
21. Greeks		22. Aboriginal Australians	
23. Egyptians		24. Vikings	
25. Aztecs		26. Maoris	
27. American Indians		28. Vikings	
29. Chinese		30. Aboriginal Australians	

Teacher's Notes

Additional Material Provided cont.

Student Information and Activity Sheets containing background information and activities related to the information.

Answers are provided at the back of the book.

Visual Review Sheet (page 9) – Students locate and colour-code each of the ancient civilizations on the world map.

Comparison and Contrast Review Sheet (page 10) – This activity allows the students to compare and contrast two different and two similar civilizations.

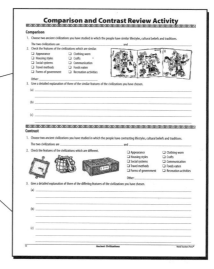

Review Sheet (page 11) – Students complete this activity which will give them a summarized overview of one of the civilizations being studied.

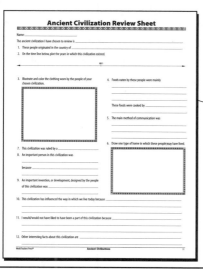

Using the Assessment Outline

Fill in the Society and Environment or English learning area.

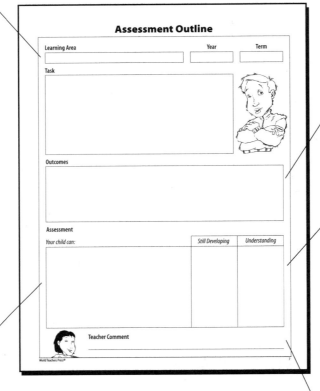

Assessment Outline

Learning Area _____ Year ___ Term ___

Task

Outcomes

Assessment

Your child can: | Still Developing | Understanding

Teacher Comment _____

Fill in the appropriate outcomes listed for the worksheet.

Complete the boxes to indicate student progress.

List the indicators assessed on the chosen worksheet.
For example; Your child can:
- Locate places on a map of Ancient Egypt.
- Summarize daily life in Ancient Egypt.
- Explain how the pyramids were constructed.

Use this space to communicate individual student's performance which can not be indicated in the formal assessment, such as work habits and particular needs or abilities.

Assessment Outline

Learning Area

Year

Term

Task

Outcomes

Assessment

Your child can:

	Still Developing	*Understanding*

Teacher Comment

Ancient Civilizations – Quiz Sheet

Name: _____ Date: _____

Answer the following questions about the ancient civilizations of the world.

1. Which civilization built the Sphinx? _____

2. Montezuma II was one of the rulers of which civilization? _____

3. Which civilization used tattoos on their face as a form of decoration? _____

4. Which civilization has beliefs called "the Dreaming"? _____

5. The Olympic Games was first developed by which civilization? _____

6. Hiram Bingham discovered the remains of the "Lost City" called Machu Picchu, which was built by which civilization? _____

7. Who wore a toga? _____

8. Which civilization built Hadrian's Wall to keep out the Scots? _____

9. Which civilization lived in homes called tepees? _____

10. Who wore a chiton or a peplon? _____

11. Which civilization built their cities along the River Nile? _____

12. Which civilization enjoyed the dance called the haka? _____

13. Who traveled in longships? _____

14. The kimono was worn by the people of which civilization? _____

15. Who ate pancakes called tortillas? _____

16. Which civilization used a quipu as a method of calculation? _____

17. Which civilization had a ruler whose name was Atahuallpa? _____

18. Which civilization used a travois attached to a horse to pull their belongings? _____

19. Who invented the Julian calendar? _____

20. Which civilization was ruled by families called dynasties? _____

21. The Acropolis and the Parthenon were built by the people of which civilization? _____

22. Which civilization of people made baskets from pandanus palm fronds? _____

23. The pharaoh was the name of the ruler of which civilization? _____

24. Which civilization of people earned a reputation as raiders and traders? _____

25. Which civilization built their city on an island in the middle of Lake Texcoco? _____

26. Spiral designs were a feature of which civilization's artwork and carvings? _____

27. To which civilization did the tribe called the Comanche belong? _____

28. Who used the runic alphabet? _____

29. Paper was invented by which civilization? _____

30. Who used a woomera to throw a spear? _____

Score: _____ /30

Visual Review of Ancient Civilizations

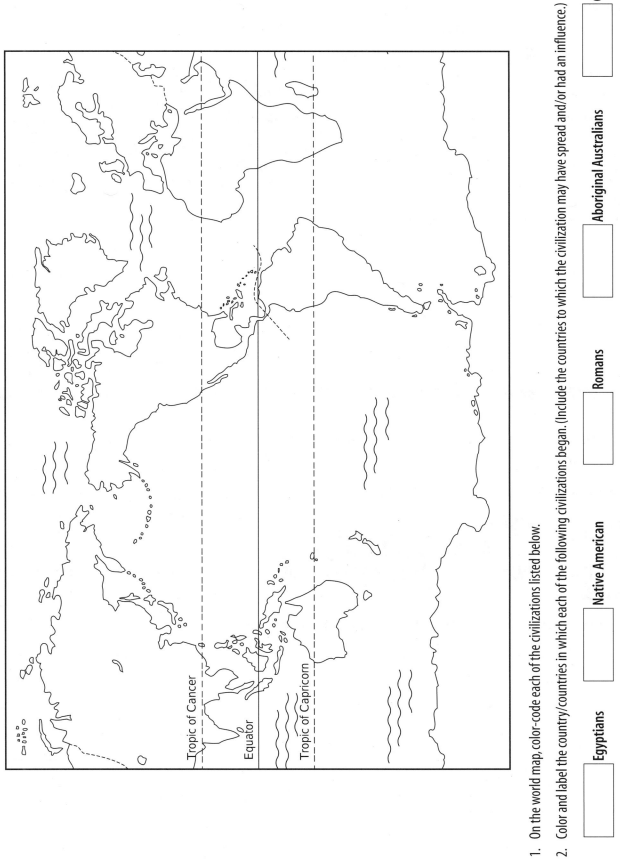

Tropic of Cancer

Equator

Tropic of Capricorn

1. On the world map, color-code each of the civilizations listed below.

2. Color and label the country/countries in which each of the following civilizations began. (Include the countries to which the civilization may have spread and/or had an influence.)

| Egyptians | Native American | Romans | Aboriginal Australians | Chinese |
| Vikings | Aztecs | Maoris | Greeks | Incas |

Comparison and Contrast Review Activity

Comparison

1. Choose two ancient civilizations you have studied in which the people have similar lifestyles, cultural beliefs and traditions.

   The two civilizations are _____ and _____.

2. Check the features of the civilizations which are similar.

   ❑ Appearance   ❑ Clothing worn
   ❑ Housing styles   ❑ Crafts
   ❑ Social systems   ❑ Communication
   ❑ Travel methods   ❑ Foods eaten
   ❑ Forms of government ❑ Recreation activities

   Other: _____

3. Give a detailed explanation of three of the similar features of the civilizations you have chosen.

   (a) _____

   _____

   (b) _____

   _____

   (c) _____

   _____

Contrast

1. Choose two ancient civilizations you have studied in which the people have contrasting lifestyles, cultural beliefs and traditions.

   The two civilizations are _____ and _____.

2. Check the features of the civilizations which are different.

   ❑ Appearance   ❑ Clothing worn
   ❑ Housing styles   ❑ Crafts
   ❑ Social systems   ❑ Communication
   ❑ Travel methods   ❑ Foods eaten
   ❑ Forms of government ❑ Recreation activities

   Other: _____

3. Give a detailed explanation of three of the differing features of the civilizations you have chosen.

   (a) _____

   _____

   _____

   (b) _____

   _____

   _____

   (c) _____

   _____

   _____

Ancient Civilization Review Sheet

Name: _____

The ancient civilization I have chosen to review is _____.

1. These people originated in the country of _____.

2. On the time line below, plot the years in which this civilization existed.

AD 1

◄───────────────────────────────┼───────────────────────────────►

3. Illustrate and color the clothing worn by the people of your chosen civilization.

4. Foods eaten by these people were mainly

   _____

   _____

   _____

   These foods were cooked by _____

5. The main method of communication was

   _____

   _____

   _____

6. Draw one type of home in which these people may have lived.

7. This civilization was ruled by a _____.

8. An important person in this civilization was

   _____

   because _____

   _____

9. An important invention, or development, designed by the people of this civilization was _____

   _____

10. This civilization has influenced the way in which we live today because _____

    _____

    _____

11. I would/would not have liked to have been a part of this civilization because _____

    _____

    _____

12. Other interesting facts about this civilization are _____

    _____

ANCIENT EGYPT

Student Information

Daily Life in Egypt

Most Egyptian families lived in huts made with dried mud bricks. Most houses had three or four rooms, but the wealthy Egyptians may have lived in houses with as many as 70 rooms. Small windows helped to keep out the sun's heat and wet mats helped to cool the air inside the houses.

Food was cooked in clay ovens or over open fires. Bread, which was made from wheat, was the main food and beer was the main drink. The Egyptians also ate a variety of fruits, such as grapes, melons, dates and figs, vegetables, fish from the Nile River, poultry, cheese and butter. They ate using their fingers.

Most Egyptians wore white linen robes. Often, a colorful shoulder-length headdress was worn. Common people wore no shoes, but wealthier Egyptians wore leather sandals. Both male and female Egyptians loved to wear jewelry and cosmetics. They outlined their eyes with eyeliner, called kohl, and wore red lip paint. Everyone liked to wear perfume, rings, earrings and necklaces.

Egyptians moved up and down the Nile River by using papyrus reed boats at first, and later, boats powered by oars. Then, around 3200 B.C., the Egyptians used sails to power their boats.

The Pyramids

The pyramids are huge stone structures with a square base, and which come to a point at the top. The Egyptians built these monuments as tombs for their kings.

The "Great Pyramid" at Giza, near Cairo, contains more than two million stone blocks. Each block weighs more than 2.3 tons. When it was built, it was 147 meters high, and the base of the pyramid covered an area of five hectares.

Because the Egyptians had no machinery, they could only have cut the blocks with very simple tools such as chisels. The blocks mostly came from quarries nearby, some came from across the Nile, while others came from as far as 200 kilometers away. Long ramps were built to drag the stones up the next layer of the pyramid. From a distance, the pyramid looked as if it had been cut from a single stone.

It has been estimated that a pyramid took many years to complete, with over 100,000 men working for three to four months each year.

Daily Life in Ancient Egypt

Ancient Egyptian peasants and farmers lived a very simple life. They lived in mud huts along the banks of the Nile River.

1. Read your information sheet and summarize the information under the following headings.

   (a) Clothing worn. _____

   _____

   (b) Foods eaten. _____

   _____

   (c) Transportation used. _____

   _____

   Discussion – *How are our lives today similar to and different from those of the Egyptians?*

   _____

   _____

ANCIENT EGYPT

About 5,000 years ago, the ancient civilization of Egypt grew and flourished along the Nile River.

Discover fascinating facts about these remarkable people as you complete the following activities.

Mapping Activity

1. Use the map of Egypt to answer these questions.

    (a) If you were sailing on a journey down the Nile, name the towns you would see, in order, from Kerma down to Tanis.

    Kerma

    _____   _____

    _____   _____

    _____   _____

    _____   _____

    _____   Tanis

    _____   _____

    (b) In which direction would you be sailing?

    _____

    (c) Name three deserts in this part of the world.

    _____   _____

    _____

    (d) Into what sea does the Nile River flow?

    _____

    (e) Name three towns near the Valley of the Kings.

    _____   _____

    _____

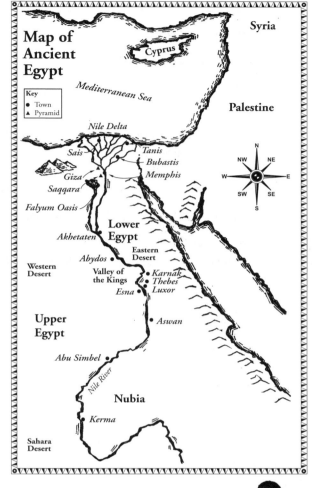

Map of Ancient Egypt

Key
- Town
▲ Pyramid

Syria

Cyprus

Mediterranean Sea

Palestine

Nile Delta

Sais

Tanis

Bubastis

Giza

Memphis

Saqqara

Falyum Oasis

Lower Egypt

Akhetaten

Eastern Desert

Western Desert

Abydos

Valley of the Kings

Karnak
Thebes
Luxor

Esna

Upper Egypt

Aswan

Abu Simbel

Nile River

Nubia

Kerma

Sahara Desert

N NW NE W E SW SE S

The Pyramids of Egypt

1. Research to find two different theories on how the pyramids were constructed.

    (a) _____

    _____

    _____

    (b) _____

    _____

    _____

Class Debate Topic: *"THE PYRAMIDS WERE BUILT BY ALIENS."*

Did You Know?

Lapis lazuli was a valuable royal blue gem originally brought from Afghanistan to Egypt by merchants. The Egyptians believed it held a special power.

1. Design a piece of jewelry which holds this special blue gemstone.

ANCIENT EGYPT

∧∧

Student Information

The Ritual of Embalming

Embalming is the process of preserving a body by the use of chemicals. The process slows down the decay so that the body appears to be lifelike for a longer period of time.

Only professional embalmers were allowed to complete the process of embalming. The internal organs were removed through surgical holes cut into the body. A powdery substance called "natron" — sodium carbonate and salt — was used to dry the inside of the body. Spices, oils and resins filled the cavities inside the body. The body was then wrapped in layers of linen strips and placed in a coffin, which was in turn placed into a tomb.

This process, which took about 70 days, is called mummification.

The Egyptians believed that preserving the body meant survival of the soul. Important Egyptians, and the Pharaohs, were mummified in this way because they believed they could enjoy life after their death.

Egyptian Words

1. Write this list of words in alphabetical order.

   (a) tomb   (a) _____

   (b) Pharaoh   (b) _____

   (c) hieroglyphs   (c) _____

   (d) scribe   (d) _____

   (e) amulet   (e) _____

   (f) sarcophagus   (f) _____

   (g) embalming   (g) _____

   (h) pyramids   (h) _____

   (i) scarabs   (i) _____

   (j) shaduf   (j) _____

   (k) barter   (k) _____

   (l) papyrus   (l) _____

   (m) sphinx   (m) _____

   (n) mummy   (n) _____

   (o) natron   (o) _____

2. Use your dictionary to find the meaning of each Egyptian-related word.

   tomb – _____

   Pharaoh – _____

   hieroglyphs – _____

   scribe – _____

   amulet – _____

   sarcophagus – _____

   embalming – _____

   pyramids – _____

   scarabs – _____

   shaduf – _____

   barter – _____

   papyrus – _____

   sphinx – _____

   mummy – _____

   natron – _____

3. Write a sentence using as many of these words as possible.

_____

_____

_____

_____

The Ritual of Embalming

Egyptians believed that the spirit of a dead person traveled to a heavenly Egypt where it would live forever. To preserve the body after death, the Egyptians developed an embalming process called mummification. The body organs, except the heart, were removed by surgery and the body was filled with a special drying substance called natron. The important organs were placed in jars and kept close to the body. The body was then wrapped in layers of cloth and placed in its coffin.

1. Briefly describe the steps involved in embalming a pharaoh's body in preparation for its trip to the afterlife.

   Step 1: _____

   _____

   Step 2: _____

   _____

   Step 3: _____

   _____

   Step 4: _____

   _____

2. Complete the missing pictures to show the process of embalming.

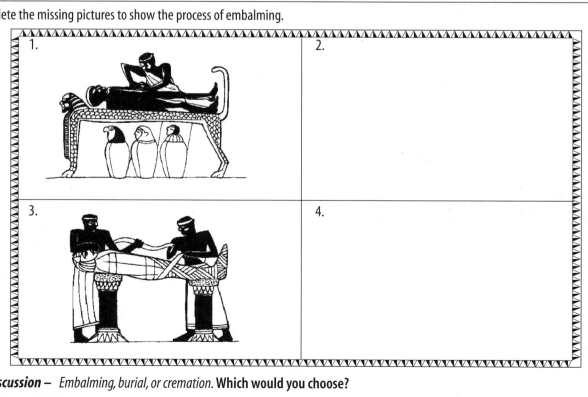

- ***Discussion –*** *Embalming, burial, or cremation.* **Which would you choose?**

Student Information

Famous Pharaohs

Tutankhamen: Became King of Egypt in 1347 B.C., at the age of nine, and died at the age of 18. His tomb is in the Valley of Kings in Egypt and was discovered by Howard Carter in 1922. It had never been opened. Items found in the tomb included jewelry, clothing, daggers, thrones, beds and linen. The treasure is now in an Egyptian Museum in Cairo. The death mask is a gold, personalized mask over the face of the mummy.

Nefertiti and Arkhenaton: Nefertiti was married to Arkhenaton and supported her husband's changes to Egyptian life in areas such as religion, art and social practices. Arkhenaton was responsible for the Armana Revolution, also the foundation of a large new capital called Arkhenaton, where carvings and paintings illustrated new styles and beliefs.

Hatshepsut: (1503 – 1472 BC) The fourth female Pharaoh, she married her half-brother, King Thutmose II. She became Queen and encouraged trade and began a vast building program. Claimed to be the god Amony's daughter.

Famous Pharaohs

Many Pharaohs (kings or queens) ruled Egypt.
They were rich and powerful.

1. Write a short profile on one of the following famous pharaohs of Egypt.

   Tutankhamen   *Nefertiti and Akhenaton*   *Hatshepsut*

   Name of Pharaoh: _____

   _____

   _____

   _____

   _____

   _____

2. In today's society, who takes the role of the pharoahs of Egypt? Explain.

ANCIENT EGYPT

Governing Egypt

Kings ruled Egypt throughout most of history. The position of Pharaoh or king was inherited (usually) by the eldest son.

The Pharaoh of Egypt was the absolute ruler. He (or she) was not obliged to obey any laws, but he needed help in ruling so he allowed other people to act for him. Most of the decisions were made by scribes.

The scribes were well educated and held great power. The vizier was a very powerful scribe and adviser to the pharaoh.

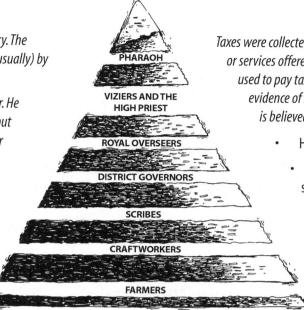

PHARAOH

VIZIERS AND THE HIGH PRIEST

ROYAL OVERSEERS

DISTRICT GOVERNORS

SCRIBES

CRAFTWORKERS

FARMERS

Taxes were collected from the farmers in the form of grain or services offered to the Pharaoh. No money was ever used to pay taxes. (There has never been any evidence of stamped money being used in Egypt. It is believed they used a bartering system.)

- Highlight the keywords.

- Discuss in a small group the similarities and differences between the Egyptian system of government and the system we use today.

1. In our system of government today, we also have a pyramid system. How is our government system similar to that of the Egyptians?

_____

_____

2. (a) What is the "barter" system? _____

_____

(b) Is it a practical system for today? Explain. _____

3. If you were born in Ancient Egypt, which position would you like to have held? Explain. _____

_____

_____

Papyrus for Paper

Papyrus was a triangular-stemmed reed which grew on the banks of the Nile River. It was overused and disappeared, but the Egyptians are trying to reintroduce it into Egypt.

1. Use the pictures to write the procedure for making paper from the papyrus plant.

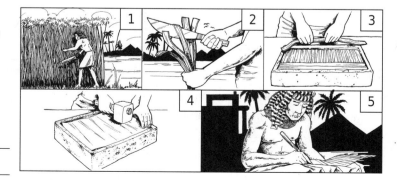

_____

_____

_____

_____

Student Information

Gods and Goddesses

The main god was the sun god *RE*, but the most important goddess was *ISIS*, who represented the devoted wife and mother. *OSIRIS* was her husband. He ruled over the vegetation and the dead. *HORIS* was their son. He was the god of the sky. He was often pictured with a falcon as his head. Many gods were pictured with the head of an animal and the body of a human.

The Sphinx

The Sphinx statue, called the "Great Sphinx," is in the desert near Giza, in Egypt, and is the largest and oldest sphinx in the world. The Egyptians built this sphinx about 4,500 years ago by carving its head and body directly out of a giant rock. They then cut stone blocks from limestone to form the front paws and legs.

The Sphinx's face is probably a portrait of Pharaoh Khafre, who may have had the monument built in his honor. His pyramid is nearby.

The Rosetta Stone

In 1799, a French officer found the stone buried in the mud near Rosetta, near Alexandria, in Egypt. It is made of black basalt. Part of the top and some of the right side are missing, and have never been found.

A French scholar named Jean François Champollion solved the riddle of the carvings on the stone. He learned the sounds of the Egyptian hieroglyphic characters and deciphered the meanings of the Egyptian words. The carvings on the stone relate to Egyptian priests commemorating the crowning of the King of Egypt from 203 B.C. to 181 B.C.

Gods and Goddess

The Egyptians worshipped hundreds of different gods and goddesses. They believed the gods influenced all aspects of nature and human activity. The most dominant god was Re (or Ra)— the sun god. Most gods were depicted with human bodies and the heads of animals.

1. Draw a picture of what you think Re (Ra) looked like.

2. Make a list of four Egyptian gods or goddesses. Draw one, and name what it represents.

Egyptian Gods/Goddesses

_____

_____

_____

_____

The Rosetta Stone

1. Research to find out the significance of:
   (a) **The Rosetta Stone**   (b) **Jean-François Champollion**

The Rosetta Stone _____

_____

_____

_____

Jean-François Champollion _____

_____

_____

_____

ANCIENT EGYPT

Sphinx

The Sphinx at Giza was carved around 4,500 years ago for the Pharaoh Khafre and guarded the way to his pyramid. However, there are many other sphinxes in Egypt.

1. Find out about the Giza Sphinx.

   (a) Where is it located? _____

   (b) Why was it built? _____

   _____

   (c) How was it built? _____

   _____

   (d) What is it made from? _____

   _____

   (e) Who was it built for? _____

   _____

Hieroglyphics

This form of writing is made up of about 750 signs or symbols of people, animals, plants and objects. It can be written left to right, or right to left.

The scribes did not rest their hand on the paper but wrote vertically.

The last priests who used this form of writing died in 400 A.D.

1. Write the words "Ancient Egypt" using these symbols.

   _____

   _____

2. Use the boxes below to design your own hieroglyphs and make your own alphabet.

ANCIENT EGYPT

Student Information

Tutankhamen

Tutankhamen became the king of Egypt when he was only nine years of age, in about 1347 B.C. Because he was so young, he would have received advice from his viziers on how to rule the kingdom of Egypt.

He is believed to have died at the age of 18, in 1339 B.C., but it is not known how he died.

His tomb was discovered by archaeologist Howard Carter, in the "Valley of Kings" in 1922. Carter had been looking for the tomb for about 10 years. He finally made the discovery when he found the entrance to the tomb had been covered by debris at the entrance of the nearby tomb of King Ramses VI.

It is the only tomb of an Egyptian king to be discovered completely untouched. The tomb had not been opened, but held over 5,000 objects including gold and carved items, jewelry, swords, trumpets, arrows and toys. A magnificent gold mask covered the head of the mummified body.

Today, most of these beautiful items are in the Egyptian Museum in Cairo.

Important Dates in Ancient Egypt's History

3100 B.C. .... Egyptian civilization began with the union of Lower and Upper Egypt.

2686 – 2181 B.C. .... The Old Kingdom was a period known for the construction of the great pyramids.

1991 B.C. .... King Amenemhet founded dynasty XII, which greatly increased Egypt's power.

1670 B.C. .... Hyksos rulers formed a dynasty that ruled Egypt for about 100 years.

1490 – 1436 B.C. .... The Egyptian empire reached its height during the reign of King Thutmose III.

1367 B.C. .... Akhenaton became king of Egypt and introduced major religious reforms.

1070 B.C. .... Dynasty XX ended and Egypt began to decline rapidly as a strong nation.

332 B.C. .... Alexander the Great added Egypt to his empire and founded the city of Alexandria.

31 B.C. .... A Roman fleet crushed an Egyptian force in the Battle of Actium, leading to Rome's take over of Egypt in 30 B.C.

A.D. 642 .... Muslims from Arabia seized Alexandria and completed their conquest of Egypt.

I Want my Mummy

1. You are an archaeologist on the verge of discovering important information about a tomb in Egypt. Write a story, poem, or play about the events leading to your discovery and the exciting events which happened during the opening of the tomb and afterwards. Plan your piece below.

    _____

    _____

    _____

    _____

    _____

2. Perform your play for your class, or read your story or poem.

ANCIENT EGYPT

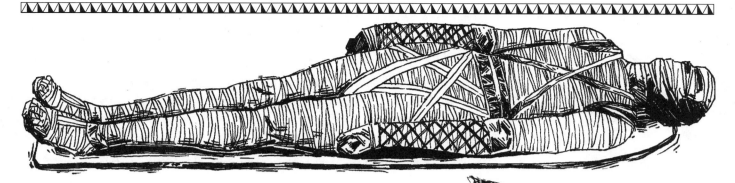

Tutankhamen

1. Research to find the answers to these questions about the Pharaoh Tutankhamen.

    (a) In about what year did Tutankhamen become King of Egypt? _____

    (b) At what age is it believed he died? _____

    (c) Where is the tomb of King Tutankhamen? _____

    (d) How old was Tutankhamen when he became king? _____

    (e) A man had been looking for many years to find the tomb of Tutankhamen.

    What was his name? _____

    (f) In which year was his discovery made? _____

    (g) Had the tomb been previously opened? _____

    (h) Describe some of the items found in the tomb. _____

    (i) What is the "death mask"? _____

    (j) Where are the objects from the tomb displayed now? _____

    (k) Draw a picture of an item from Tutankhamen's tomb in the box provided.

Time for History

The Egyptian civilization began about 3100 B.C., with two kingdoms—Lower Egypt in the north and Upper Egypt in the south.

King Menes conquered Lower Egypt and united the country by forming the first national government. He established the first of 30 Egyptian dynasties.

Egyptian history can be divided into three main parts:

1. ***The Old Kingdom*** (or Pyramid Age)
2. ***The Middle Kingdom***
3. ***The New Kingdom*** (the Golden Age)

---

1. Construct a time line to show the development of the Egyptians over the past 5,000 years.

3,000 B.C.	2,000 B.C.	1,000 B.C.	A.D. 1	A.D. 1,000	A.D. 2,000

Looking for more information? Use the Internet and these keywords:

Ancient Egypt   *pharaohs*   *Tutankhamen*   *hieroglyphics*   *embalming*   *papyrus*

THE VIKINGS

Who were the Vikings?

The Vikings lived in the Scandinavian countries of Norway, Denmark and Sweden. They lived peacefully as farmers, craftsmen and merchants until the late 8th century, when they took to the sea in search of new land and wealth. For the next 300 years, Viking raiding parties terrorized Europe and Britain with their violent raids on wealthy towns.

Complete the activities to discover the fascinating facts about how these people lived.

Iceland

North Sea

British Isles

Norway

Sweden

Denmark

Russia

Volga River

Dnieper River

Atlantic Ocean

France

Black Sea

Spain

Mediterranean Sea

Map of Viking Voyages

THE VIKINGS

Why did the Vikings become raiders?

1. Choose the correct word to complete these sentences.

builders	monks	population	raid
looted	invaded	fertile	first
destroyed	fished	animals	east
scarce	island	treasures	sailed

Because Scandinavia was never _____ by the Romans, the people and their culture thrived. The

_____ increased, farmers grew crops and kept _____, hunted for seal

and deer, and _____ the sea. However, farmland was becoming _____ and there

was not enough _____ land for the growing population.

The Vikings were experienced ship_____ and they _____ in their longboats to

_____ nearby lands. They returned to their homes with their ships loaded with _____ and

slaves. The _____ known Viking raid was in 793 A.D. on the monastery on the _____ of

Lindisfarne on the _____ coast of England. The Vikings slaughtered the _____,

_____ the church and _____ its treasures.

2. Instead of raiding neighboring countries, can you think of a more peaceful solution for the Vikings?

_____

_____

_____

_____

_____

_____

Where did the Vikings come from?

1. The Vikings came from the countries of

   N_____,

   S_____ and

   D_____.

2. Color these countries in red on the map on page 22.

3. The Vikings sailed vast distances to raid, trade and explore. Name six places the Vikings visited.

   _____ _____

   _____ _____

   _____ _____

4. Color these places in green.

What did the Vikings wear?

1. These pictures show the traditional clothing worn by men and women. Choose one of the pictures below to enlarge and color.

Use a separate sheet of paper for your picture.

THE VIKINGS

Viking Time Line

1. Complete the time line using the following information about Vikings. Write the information in chronological order.

845 – Vikings capture the Spanish cities of Seville and Cordoba. Paris in France and Hamburg in Germany are also attacked and plundered.

890 – Large Viking raiding fleet enters the Mediterranean Sea.

795 – Vikings attack monasteries on Iona in west Scotland and on the west coast of Ireland.

862 – Rurik, a Swedish Viking, occupies the city of Novgorod in Russia.

994 – A fleet of 94 Viking ships from Norway and Sweden attacks London, England.

866 – Large Viking force lands in England looking for land to settle, and captures York, in northeast England.

1013 – A Danish King, Svein Forkbeard, invades England with his son, Cnut.

1100 – Close of the Viking age as Viking settlers are absorbed into the local communities.

793 – Vikings from Norway attack and destroy the monastery on the island of Lindisfarne, on the northeast coast of England.

1016 – King Cnut of Denmark becomes King of all England until 1035.

843 – Danish Vikings attack Nantes and Toulouse in France.

1066 – Last great Viking ruler, Harald Hardraada, invades England, but is defeated at the Battle of Hastings, near York.

793 –
1100 –

Viking Invasions

1. List of all the places mentioned above which the Vikings are known to have attacked.

_____

_____

_____

_____

Questions to Ponder

Can you find logical answers to these questions?

1. What distances did the Vikings travel over the seas?
2. How could they have cooked or eaten their food?
3. How could they wash themselves or their clothes?
4. What could they have done to keep their minds occupied while they were rowing?
5. How did they navigate during the day and at night?
6. Where did they put the slaves and jewels when returning home?

THE VIKINGS

Viking "Longships"

1. Find the words in this passage to fit the boxes below. All words run vertically to complete the puzzle.

The Vikings were renowned sailors and traveled all over the northern world in their longships. The Viking raiding ships were called Drakkar, or "Longships," and were built by expert craftsmen. Pine, fir and oak timbers were most commonly used to build the boats. They were long and narrow—up to 30 meters or more in length and 5 meters wide—and with a very shallow draft. This meant the boats could ride the ocean waves and sail inland up rivers. The keel was made from a single tree trunk to give the boat strength and flexibility in storms. The figurehead on the prow of the boat was often a carved dragon's head and brightly painted. Viking shields lined the sides of the boat.

| l | o | n | g | s | h | i | p | s |

2. Color this picture of a longship. Some things are missing—draw them in your picture!

   (a) Brightly colored and striped sails.
   (b) Shields lining the sides.
   (c) A dragon's head on the prow of the boat.
   (d) Fresh drinking water stored in barrels.
   (e) A treasure chest filled with looted treasure.

Viking Crafts and Jewelry

The Vikings were expert metal craftsmen and made beautiful jewelry from gold and silver. Tunic brooches were worn by the women. Men and women wore rings on their fingers and arms. Necklaces were often made from pottery, glass and crystal beads and coins. Buckles, coatpins and pendants were also worn.

1. On the back of this page, design and illustrate a piece of jewelry which the Vikings may have worn.

Viking Levels of Society

1. Read the following passage and label the pictures above correctly.
   Viking society was divided into several levels. At the top was the King, who protected his people and led his army into battle. Noblemen, called "Jarls," advised the King, collected the taxes and helped the King maintain the laws. Below the Jarls were the "Karls" or freemen. These men were warriors, farmers, craftsmen, or traders. At the bottom of Viking society were the "Thralls" or slaves. Thralls were the men who had been captured during raids and sold for profit.

2. **Collaborative Discussion**: Form groups of 4.
   Each group member is either the King, a Jarl, a Karl, or a Thrall. Your task is to convince the other members of your group that your position in Viking society is the best level to be living in.

Student Information

Famous Vikings

King Cnut II (Canute)

Canute was the son of Svein Forkbeard, the Danish king. He conquered England in A.D. 1013. After the death of his father and a struggle with the English, he defeated the Londoners at Essex and became King of England in 1016. He ruled wisely and divided England into four earldoms. In 1019, he also became King of Denmark, and in 1028, the King of Norway. He ruled these countries until his death in 1035.

Eric the Red

It is thought that Eric the Red was born in 950, in Southern Norway. He was called Eric the Red because of his red hair. When he was about 10 years old, he moved with his father to Iceland. He explored the waters west of Iceland, reached the east coast of a large landmass and traveled around the southern tip to the west coast. He named the new land Greenland to attract people to it.

In about 985, Eric sailed for Greenland again and, with 450 people, established two settlements in this new land. He was the leader of both settlements. He died about A.D. 1000.

Leif Ericson

Leif Ericson was a Norwegian explorer who was born about 980. He was the son of Eric the Red, who had earlier established the first settlements in Greenland.

Ericson was born in Iceland, but moved with his father to Greenland when he was about five years old.

In 1002, he sailed west from Greenland to look for land, which had been sighted by a sea captain. He discovered this land, sailed south and found grapes growing on the land. He named the land Vinland (Wineland). It is thought that this land he discovered was on the east coast of Canada. Ericson spent the winter in Vinland, then returned to Greenland. After his father's death, he stayed to govern the settlement.

Famous Vikings

1. Use the information sheet and your own research to write a report about one of these famous Vikings:

   King Cnut (Canute)   Leif Ericson   Eric the Red

   _____

   _____

   _____

   _____

   _____

   _____

   _____

   _____

   _____

   _____

   _____

   _____

   _____

THE VIKINGS

Vikings at Home

The Viking family homes were called "long houses" because of their rectangular shape. The walls were made of wood and the overhanging roof was made of turf to keep in the warmth. In the center of each house a fire burned constantly. Above the fire hung a large pot, or cauldron, used for cooking. Family members gathered in the main hall around the fire. Benches around the walls were used to sit and sleep on. Food was stored in wooden tubs, and valuables were locked in chests.

1. Use the information to illustrate what you think the inside of a long house would have looked like.

2. Are there any similarities to the way your family lives?   **YES**   **NO**

3. (a) Compare and contrast your lifestyle to the ways in which the Vikings lived.

Compare (Similarities)	Contrast (Differences)

(b) Which lifestyle do you prefer? Explain why. _____

_____

4. What might this have been used for?

_____

5. What might these have been used for?

_____

6. What might be inside this chest?

7. How might this meat have been cooked?

_____

8. What may have been in this jug?

_____

Viking Women

While the Viking men were raiding other countries, the Viking women had many duties at home. They had to harvest the crops, and look after the sheep, oxen, geese and chickens, the children and the elderly. In the home, the women cooked the food, baked the bread and made cheese and butter. They spent many hours spinning and weaving wool or linen to make clothes and blankets for their families. Remedies for the sick and elderly were mixed by the women who were caring for them. As a sign of responsibility, the women always carried their keys with them. These keys were for the door of her home, to the strongbox or to chests containing precious jewels or silks.

1. Do women in today's society have specific duties?   **YES**   **NO**

Explain. _____

_____

2. Make a list of all the duties of a Viking woman.

3. Check which of these duties on the list can still be the responsibility of women in today's society.

Duties	Check

THE VIKINGS

Viking Words

Many words we use in English today come from the Vikings.
Make up a poem using some of these "Viking" words.

landscape	skate	curtain	freckles	tight	score	scarf	tree	sale	keel
rugged	penny	law	bone	seat	sky	soap	kid	food	skirt
purse	steer	toy	grow	cup	thread	sweat	murky		

| **Tuesday** | **Wednesday** | **Thursday** | **Friday** |
| *Tyr's day; god of war* | *Woden's day; god of wisdom, war (Woden is also known as Odin)* | *Thor's day; god of thunder* | *Freya's day; goddess of love* |

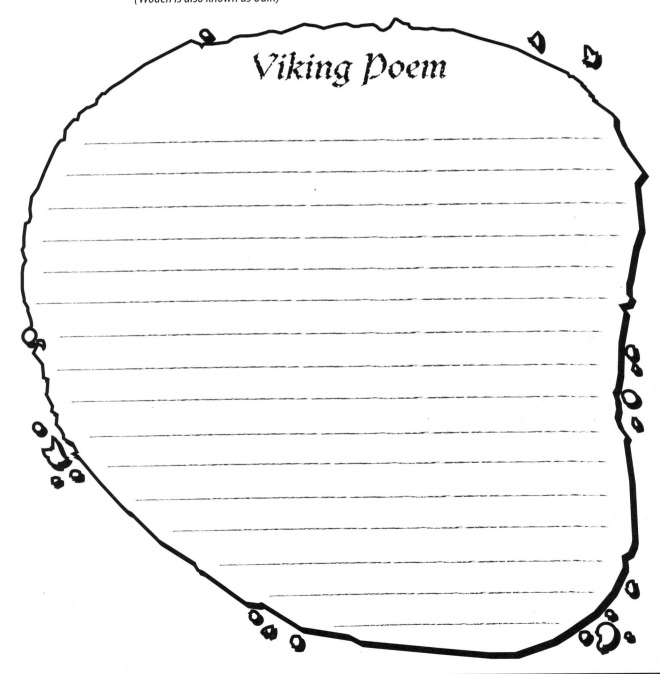

Viking Poem

THE VIKINGS

Runic Alphabet

The Vikings had their own alphabet. The letters in the alphabet are called "runes." Runes were cut with a sharp point, or knife, onto stone, wood, bone, or metal. All the runes have straight sides.

| f | u | th | a | r | k | g | w | h | n | i | y | ei | p | z | s | t | b | e | m | l | ng | d | o |

1. Use the letters in the runic alphabet to write the following words.

   (a) ship _____

   (b) raid _____

   (c) shield _____

   (d) prow _____

   (e) Sweden _____

   (f) looted _____

Menu for a Viking Feast

Fish soup (haddock)

Seagull eggs

Sausage stuffed with blood and lard, and meat spiced with thyme and garlic

Smoked mutton

Dried cod eaten with butter

Stew with peas, beans, parsnips, carrots and veal; flavored with coriander

Spit-roasted boar coated in butter and dill

Game stew with hare, seagull and cormorant; flavored with cumin

Cheese

Wild berries

Apples

Condiments; salt and mustard

Drinks: ale, mead, wine, milk

---

1. (a) Choose one scrumptious dish from the "Menu for a Viking Feast."
   Write the procedure you would use to prepare one of these delicious dishes.

   (b) Combine your dish with others to make a complete Viking feast.

   Step 1 _____

   _____

   _____

   _____

   _____

   _____

   _____

   _____

   _____

   _____

   _____

   _____

   _____

Looking for more information? Try the Internet and these keywords.

Scandinavia   longships   runes   Vikings   Eric the Red

Student Information

Transportation

The American Plains Indians used a travois to transport their possessions and people from place to place when they moved their camps. A large travois was often pulled by a horse or a dog, but the smaller version could be dragged by a person.

The travois consisted of two wooden poles which were attached to a frame and pulled along the ground.

Mapping Activity

Complete the following.

1. Color the oceans and seas blue.

2. Name the oceans and seas surrounding North America.

   _____   _____

   _____   _____

3. Name the four physical features which border the area known as the Great Plains.

   _____   _____

   _____   _____

THE NATIVE AMERICANS

Who were the Native Americans?

The ancestors of the Native Americans were thought to have come from northeast Asia over 20,000 years ago.

In order to survive, the Native Americans adapted to the environment in which they lived—hot deserts, thick forests, deep valleys and flat treeless prairies. They became hunters, trappers and farmers and made the best use of the resources the environment offered.

By the time Christopher Columbus arrived in North America in 1492, over 300 tribes had spread across the vast continent.

The following activities will concentrate mainly on the lives of the tribes of Native Americans living on the Great Plains. Complete them to find out more about these fascinating people.

Who were the tribes of the Great Plains?

About 20 different tribes of Native Americans lived on the Great Plains. Some tribes were nomadic and some settled in villages.

1. Can you place the correct name from the list given into the correct position on the pole?

NATIVE AMERICAN TRIBES

Arapaho
Mandan
Plains
Cree
Sioux
Oglala
Hidatsa
Crow
Apache
Cheyenne
Assinboin
Lakota
Kiowa
Kutenai
Pawnee
Black Feet
Shoshoni
Comanche

Native American Words

1. Which one letter of the alphabet can be used to complete each of these words below?

_____

e	t	r	o	g	l	y		h
a		o	o	s	e			
a	r	f	l	e	c	h	e	
e	m	m	i	c	a	n		
e	a	c	e	■		i		e
o	w	w	o	w				
r	a	i	r	i	e	s		

2. What does each of these words mean? Use your dictionary. Write your answers on a separate piece of paper.

Do You Know?

- What was a travois?   • Why was it used?   • How was it used?   • What pulled the travois?

1. A travois was _____

_____

_____

_____

www.worldteacherspress.com   **Ancient Civilizations**

THE NATIVE AMERICANS

Student Information

Procedure to Erect a Tepee

The Plains Indians built cone-shaped structures called tepees, which were easily portable and quickly erected or taken down when the tribe moved camp. The tepees were erected by standing several poles on end, and tying them together at the top. Buffalo skins were then placed around the outside of the pole frame to cover the outside of the tepee. A hole was left at the top of the poles to allow ventilation.

It was the women's job to erect the tepee, and the opening of the tepee always faced towards the rising sun in the east.

Grass Lodges

Some Plains Indians built grass lodges for their shelter. These were made by building a wooden frame and then covering it with cut grasses and cane or reeds.

---

1. Use these pictures to write the procedure used to erect a tepee.

THE NATIVE AMERICANS

What types of homes did the Native Americans live in?

Most Native Americans living on the Plains lived in big cone-shaped tents called tipis (or tepees). These portable homes were built around a framework of long wooden poles. The door of the tepee always faced the east, towards the rising sun. It was the women's job to put the tepee up and take it down again when the tribe moved location.

1. What were grass lodges?

   _____

   _____

   _____

   _____

2. Construct a model tepee of your own using wooden sticks and cloth.

Nomadic Tribes

1. Why do you think some tribes were nomadic while other tribes settled in one place?

   _____

   _____

   _____

   _____

2. Can you name a group, or groups, of people today who might lead a "nomadic" life?

   _____

   _____

   _____

3. Make a list of ten things you might not need if you were leading a nomadic life.

   _____   _____

   _____   _____

   _____   _____

   _____   _____

4. Discuss and list some advantages and disadvantages of a nomadic life.

   _____

   _____

3. List four items which may have been inside a tepee and briefly explain what each may have been used for.

   (i) _____

   (ii) _____

   (iii) _____

   (iv) _____

How were the children educated?

1. Read the passage below about how the children of the Plains Indians learned about life.

Children did not attend school, but learned about survival, life and their culture by listening to and copying their parents. Boys were taught hunting and riding skills. Girls were taught household tasks, beadwork, embroidery and painting.

2. Describe how your education is similar to and different from the way the Plains Indian children learned.

My education is ...

similar because

   _____

   _____

   _____

   _____

different because _____

   _____

   _____

   _____

Student Information

Time Line of Important Events

About 15,000 years ago it is thought that early hunters and gatherers migrated across the Bering Strait from Asia, by means of an Ice-age bridge from Asia to North America.

These Stone Age people settled on the grassy plains of central Canada, then moved south to Mexico and west to the Rocky Mountains. Most lived in villages along streams and rivers where they could catch fish for food.

From 850 A.D., farming areas were established into the Great Plains, along the Missouri River, where the soil was rich, and the buffalo were plentiful.

In 1492, Christopher Columbus arrived on American shores and claimed the land for the Spanish.

The Spaniards settled in parts of North America, and brought with them horses, guns and steel knives, all which were greatly prized by the Native Americans who traded for them. But they also brought diseases, such as smallpox, which killed many Native Americans. The Spanish also took the land from the Native Americans and claimed it as their own. Buffalo herds were wiped out by widespread killing. By 1890, the herds had almost disappeared.

The Native Americans did not like what was happening and they fought for their land, with many lives being lost in the process. The government allocated land for the Native Americans, called reservations. The Native Americans' land was taken by the white European settlers to become cattle ranches and homesteads. As in other countries, this "invasion" caused widespread conflict and enduring mistrust.

Clothing

Many Native Americans made their clothes from the skins and fur of animals such as deer, elk, caribou, buffalo and rabbit.

The common clothing style was a tunic, which was longer for women and shorter for men. The tunic had detachable sleeves. Leggings were also worn. These protected the legs and kept them warm. The Native Americans adorned themselves with flowers, beads and feathers and on special occasions painted themselves and their clothes with intricate designs.

Moccasins were worn on their feet. These were a soft type of leather slipper, or shoe, made from buffalo hide, with a combined sole and heel.

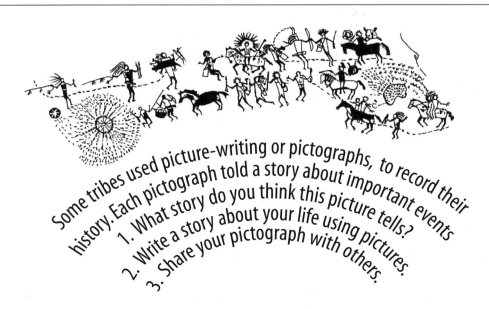

Some tribes used picture-writing or pictographs, to record their history. Each pictograph told a story about important events.
1. What story do you think this picture tells?
2. Write a story about your life using pictures.
3. Share your pictograph with others.

THE NATIVE AMERICANS

Time Line of Important Events

Write brief answers to the following questions.

1. When did the ancestors of the Native Americans arrive in North America? What route could they have taken?

2. Where did these people first settle?

3. When did they move to the area known as the Great Plains? Why did these people settle in this area?

4. Who arrived in America in 1492? Why?

5. What items were traded? What significance would these have had on their lives?

6. What influences, good and bad, did the white settlers have on the Plains tribes?

7. What are reservations? How did they come about?

Answers:

1. _____
_____

2. _____
_____

3. _____
_____

4. _____
_____

5. _____
_____

6. _____
_____

7. _____
_____

Communication with Pictographs

The picture on the previous page tells a story of

_____
_____
_____
_____
_____
_____

My Pictograph

What did the Native Americans wear?

This picture shows typical clothing worn by tribes on the Great Plains.
Research Activity: Answer the following questions to find out more about what they wore.

1. From what materials did they make their clothing?

_____
_____

2. What did the Native Americans wear on their feet? What were they made of?

_____
_____

3. What use were leggings?

_____
_____

For special occasions, everyday clothes were painted.

4. How did they decorate their clothes?

_____
_____

Student Information

Pemmican

Pemmican is dried, lean meat which has been pounded into a paste with melted fat, then pressed into cakes and cooked. Sometimes berries, roots and seeds were added. Pemmican was an important food among certain tribes of Native Americans.

What did the Plains Indians eat?

The foods below are some of those eaten by the Plains Indians.

1. Can you find them in this word search?

dried meat	*herbs*
elk	*rabbits*
pumpkins	*fish*
pemmican	*moose*
deer	*strawberries*
turnips	*plums*
maize	*squash*
buffalo meat	*beans*
berries	*sunflowers*

y	t	a	e	m	d	e	i	r	d	a	s
e	w	t	u	r	n	i	p	s	i	t	a
z	h	e	s	a	i	l	a	t	t	a	o
i	s	v	e	b	c	s	n	r	p	e	e
a	u	c	s	b	o	n	t	a	e	m	t
m	n	a	o	i	d	a	l	w	m	o	w
y	f	i	o	t	o	é	a	b	m	l	p
p	l	u	m	s	d	b	e	e	i	a	u
e	o	t	s	b	h	c	h	r	c	f	m
f	w	n	i	d	m	i	r	r	a	f	p
a	e	l	k	r	k	r	f	i	n	u	k
h	r	t	b	e	r	r	i	e	s	b	i
l	s	t	h	s	a	u	q	s	o	l	n
g	t	i	e	w	c	n	h	e	r	b	s

2. What is pemmican?

_____

_____

THE NATIVE AMERICANS

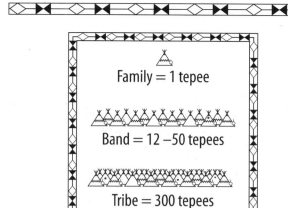

Family = 1 tepee

Band = 12 – 50 tepees

Tribe = 300 tepees

What was the family structure of the Plains Indians?

1. How many Plains Indians would form a band?

   _____

2. How many Plains Indians would form a tribe?

   _____

3. What is the equivalent to a tribe and band in our society? (Think about suburbs, countries, cities.)

   Tribe _____ Band _____

4. Make a list of the family members who may have lived in each tepee.

   _____   _____

   _____   _____

   _____   _____

   _____   _____

How were the tribes governed?

Fill in the missing words.

allowed	pipe	final	Plains
Important	chief	meetings	chosen
governed	opinions		

Why were the buffalo hunted?

The buffalo provided the Plains Indians with almost everything they needed for their existence.

1. Unjumble the words below.
   Each word is a part of the buffalo used by Native Americans.

2. Find the right space for each word in the puzzle below.

   rhia _____

   tame _____

   verli _____

   nudg _____

   tfa _____

   dhies _____

   fohos _____

   ruf _____

   rohns _____

   nebos _____

   t
   h
   e
   ■
   b
   u
   f
   f
   a
   l
   o

3. Which one of these buffalo parts do you think was the most important? _____

Crafts of the Plains Indians

Women created beautiful paintings, beadwork and embroidery.

1. Enlarge this beadwork pattern and color brightly.

2. Design a pattern of your own.

3. Paint or bead your pattern using bright colors.

The _____ Indian tribes _____ their people in a democratic manner. Each band of Native Americans chose a _____ to represent their people. This leader was _____ for his bravery, wisdom and generosity. _____ decisions were made by the chiefs when they sat at _____ called tribal councils. A peace _____ was smoked in silence before discussions began. All men were _____ to voice their _____ before _____ decisions were made.

THE NATIVE AMERICANS

Student Information

Geronimo (1829 – 1909)
This Native American was a member of the Chiricahua Apache tribe. His name meant "The Smart One."

In 1877, the U.S. Government moved the Apache people to a reservation in Arizona. But the Apaches did not want to go and wars broke out between the Native Americans and the U.S. troops. Geronimo was captured and returned to the reservation.

For many years throughout Mexico, Geronimo led bloody battles against the U.S. Government's military in retaliation for army massacres of his people. In 1886, after successfully avoiding capture by 5,000 troops, Geronimo finally surrendered.

He was sent to Florida with his people as "punishment," then finally to a reservation in Oklahoma in 1894, where he lived for the rest of his life.

Sitting Bull (1834 – 1890)
Sitting Bull was the leader of the Hunkpapa Sioux tribe. After showing bravery in a fight against the Crow tribe, he was given the name Sitting Bull. In 1867, Sitting Bull, now a famous warrior and medicine man, became the chief of the entire Sioux nation.

He was promised by the U.S. government that the Black Hills of Dakota would forever belong to the Sioux. But in the mid 1870s gold was discovered there and the government ordered the Sioux to stay on their reservation. Sitting Bull refused and defeated the U.S. army in two important battles, including the Battle of the Little Big Horn.

He was forced to flee to Canada but was captured in 1881. In 1890, Sitting Bull was killed when his warriors tried to stop him from being taken away by the government.

Crazy Horse (1844 – 1877)
Crazy Horse was a chief of the Oglala Sioux. He was brave, wise, quiet — a true Native American warrior.

In 1875, the tribe was ordered by the U.S. Government to enter a reservation. But they refused, and in 1876 the cavalry attacked a Cheyenne village by mistake. Crazy Horse took revenge, and with the Sioux and the Cheyenne attacked the cavalry in the Battle of the Rosebud and the Battle of the Little Big Horn. He was killed in 1877 by a soldier in Nebraska after being tricked by the army into going unarmed into an army fort. He was buried in a secret place known only to his people.

Personality Profiles

Write a words and phrases that describe the personality and life of each of these important Native Americans.

Geronimo

_____

_____

_____

Sitting Bull

_____

_____

Crazy Horse

_____

_____

_____

THE NATIVE AMERICANS

Fun and Games for Native Americans

The Native Americans loved to dance, listen to stories and play games in their spare time. Tribal gatherings were a time for contests and games for young and old.

1. Can you match these activities with their correct endings to complete some of the activities enjoyed by the Native Americans?

pony •	• rolling
archery •	• lacrosse
hoop and ball •	• and skating
playing •	• contests
tobogganing •	• games
dice rolling •	• field hockey
listening to •	• racing
playing •	• stories and legends

2. Draw a picture in the box below of Native American children playing one of these games.

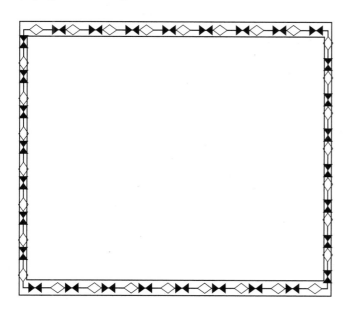

Looking for more information? Try the Internet using these keywords.

nomads	tepee (tipi)	moccasins	travois
buffalo	Geronimo	reservation	

Festivals and Ceremonies

Many festivals were held to celebrate important events. The Sun Dance was the greatest ceremony.

1. Why do you think the sun was so important to the Native Americans?

_____

_____

Men painted their faces with bright colors and wore special costumes and ornaments.

2. Draw a ceremony costume.

The Green Corn Dance is held to thank the spirit for the sun which has ripened the corn.

3. Make a list of ways in which the corn may have been used for food.

_____ _____

_____ _____

During a drought, a rainmaker performs a dance to ask the spirits for rain for crops and animals.

4. Why do you think the rainmaker's dance may have brought rain?

_____

_____

Poetry

The Native Americans lost their land and their culture as the white settlers took over. What do you think the words of this song mean?

"A Warrior _____

I have been _____

Now _____

it is all over _____

A hard time _____

I have." _____

_____

Sitting Bull _____

THE AZTECS

Student Information

Tenochtitlan

In 1325, the Aztecs were guided to the site of their capital city by the god, Huitzilopochtli. They chose to build their city in the center of a shallow, swampy lake called Texcoco.

Three causeways, made of raised earth, were built to connect the city to the mainland. A grid system of canals and streets was constructed around pyramids, temples and palaces. These huge limestone structures dominated the landscape. The canals were used to transport people and goods around the city, using boats. Dams were built to protect the city from floods.

The city of Tenochtitlan flourished with the people growing their own food in chinampas, which were "island gardens" formed by piling up the mud to create the soil to grow their crops. The Aztecs made their homes from adobe (clay), reeds, or stone.

By 1519, the great market was attracting up to 60,000 people daily. In the center of the city was the Great Temple, which was built in honor of the god Huitzilopochtli. This temple was used for religious ceremonies.

The Spanish conqueror, Hernán Cortés, captured the city in 1521 and destroyed it. Mexico City is built on the ruins of this once great city.

Research Activity

Read the information, then answer the questions to find out how this great city survived and thrived.

1. How was the island of Tenochtitlan connected to the mainland? What were these made of?

   _____

   _____

   _____

2. How did the Aztecs travel through their city?

   _____

   _____

   _____

3. What sort of homes did they live in?

   _____

   _____

4. What buildings were in the center of the city?

   _____

   _____

   _____

5. What were "chinampas"? How did they build them?

   _____

   _____

   _____

   _____

6. What was this building called? Where was it situated? What was it used for? What was used to build it?

   _____

   _____

   _____

   _____

   _____

   _____

   _____

   _____

Color the Pacific Ocean and Gulf of Mexico blue.

Who were the Aztecs?

A wandering tribe of hunters called the Tenochas, later known as the Aztecs, settled in the Valley of Mexico in A.D. 1300.

The Aztecs chose to build their city, known as Tenochtitlan, on a small, marshy island on Lake Texcoco.

The thriving city of Tenochtitlan became the Aztec's capital city, and in only 200 years the Aztecs had grown into a powerful civilization.

How did the Aztecs build such a strong civilization if they lived on an island in a lake? Find the answer, and more, about these fascinating people by completing the activities.

The Aztec City of Tenochtitlan

According to Aztec legend, the god, Huitzilopochtli, told the tribe to search for "a swamp where an eagle sits on a cactus with a snake in its claws," and it was here that their city should be built. The Aztecs found this site on a swampy island in the middle of a shallow lake in the Valley of Mexico, Lake Texcoco.

Mapping Activity

Use the map above to find the answers to the following questions.

1. Name the lake which surrounds Tenochtitlan.

   _____

2. Which mountain is close by this lake?

   _____

3. Vera Cruz is on the coast of the

   _____

4. Name five towns/cities in the Valley of Mexico.

   _____

   _____

   _____

   _____

   _____

THE AZTECS

Student Information

Montezuma II

Montezuma II was born in 1480, and was the great-grandson of the Aztec Emperor, Montezuma I.

He was the Emperor of the Aztec empire when the Spaniards arrived. He ruled from 1502 until 1520. During that time he built many temples, waterways and hospitals, but he taxed the people heavily, and was not popular.

When Hernán Cortés arrived in Tenochtitlan in 1519, Montezuma II welcomed him, and gave him gifts of gold and jewelry. Later, Cortés captured the city and held Montezuma II as a hostage. Montezuma II was stoned to death in 1520.

Order in Aztec Society

The Kings (Tlatoani) were assisted by their deputies (Cihuacoat). Priests and scribes were well educated. Government officials were from noble families. Warriors and knights were held in high esteem for their bravery. Then came the farmers, craftsmen and traders. Slaves were at the bottom of Aztec society.

1.   *Complete the pictures using the corresponding pictures above.*

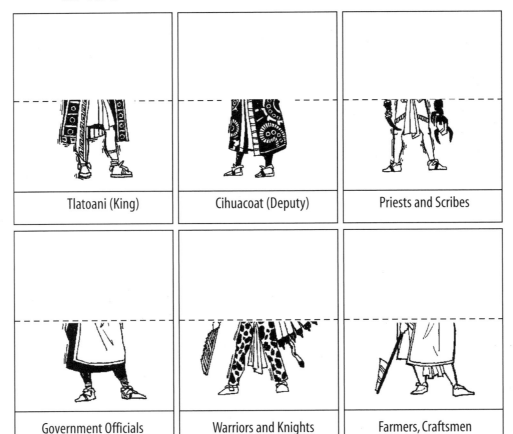

| Tlatoani (King) | Cihuacoat (Deputy) | Priests and Scribes |
| Government Officials | Warriors and Knights | Farmers, Craftsmen |

THE AZTECS

Time line of Important Aztec Events

1. Read the passage below. Use the information to complete the time line, recording the important events in Aztec history.

It was A.D. 1200 when the nomadic tribe called the Aztecs reached the Valley of Mexico. By 1325, the Aztecs had finally settled on the island of Tenochtitlan. Seventy-five years later, this tribe had conquered most of the other tribes in the Valley of Mexico. They had become the strongest civilization in the Valley of Mexico by the year 1500. Two years later, the reign of the last Aztec ruler, Montezuma II, had begun. In 1519, the Spanish army, led by Hernán Cortés, arrived in Mexico. Cortés and his army killed Montezuma II in 1520. One year later, Cortés returned to Tenochtitlan and defeated the Aztecs in a great battle, then demolished the city. The Aztec Empire was destroyed and Spanish rule began.

A.D. 1200 _____

_____

_____

_____

_____

_____

_____

A.D. 1521 _____

_____

Profile of an Aztec Ruler: Montezuma II

Write a profile of the life and times of Montezuma II.

1. Born: _____

2. Who was he? _____

_____

3. Time of rule: _____

4. What did he do? Why didn't people like him? _____

_____

5. Death—how did he die? _____

_____

THE AZTECS

What did the Aztecs wear?

1. Write two similarities and two differences in the clothing worn by the wealthy Aztecs and that worn by poorer Aztecs.

Similarities: _____

_____

_____

_____

Differences: _____

_____

_____

_____

2. Why do you think the wealthy Aztecs wore more colorful and decorative clothing?

_____

_____

_____

_____

What did the Aztecs eat?

The Aztecs' main food was a grain called maize. Pancakes, called tortillas, were made from maize dough and cooked on a hot surface. Very little meat was eaten, but occasionally the Aztecs ate turkey or duck—and even dog. However, many fruits and vegetables were grown and eaten, and these provided a healthy diet for the Aztecs.

Tortillas

450 g plain flour
1 tsp baking powder
1 tsp salt
1 tbsp fat
175 mL cold water

Mix the flour, baking powder and salt together, then rub in the fat until the mixture looks like breadcrumbs. Add the water and mix to a dough. Make a dozen balls and roll them out on a floured surface. Grill or fry them very quickly and add any filling you like.

1. Can you unjumble these foods eaten by Aztecs?

smatoteo _____

mukpnip _____

snabe _____

perpeps _____

rotacrs _____

stapneu _____

voodaca _____

swete rocn _____

etesw toptao _____

lilhci _____

Aztec Warriors and Wars

1. Write the antonyms for the words in bold print in the passage below. Then rewrite the passage on a separate piece of paper.

*Aztec warriors were taught when they were very **old** about fighting, weapons and warfare. Only **girls** were trained to fight, and it was a duty and a **disgrace** to fight in a battle. Aztec warriors attacked neighboring tribes attempting to **return** their crops and animals. They **released** prisoners to use as human sacrifices to the gods. The courage, **cowardice** and **weakness** of these **timid** warriors helped to **demolish** their Empire, and establish them as the **weakest** of all of the tribes in the valley.*

old	_____	girls	_____
disgrace	_____	released	_____
cowardice	_____	weakness	_____
timid	_____	demolish	_____
weakness	_____	return	_____

2. How many words can you make using these letters?

_____

_____

_____

e	w	r	t
r	a	i	c
z	r	a	o

_____

_____

_____

3. These letters spell . . .

____ ____ ____ ____ ____   ____ ____ ____ ____ ____ ____

Did You Know?

*The Aztecs used the cacao bean to make chocolate, which they called **chocolatl**. Only the rich Aztecs could afford it!*

1. Research to find out how the Aztecs made their chocolate from the cacao bean.

_____

_____

_____

Student Information

Huitzilopochtli

Huitzilopochtli was the major Aztec god. He was represented by pictures of an armed warrior with a helmet covered in hummingbird feathers. He was the god of the sun and war, encouraging his people to fight the enemy bravely and without mercy.

Quetzalcoatl

Represented as a feathered serpent, Quetzalcoatl was the god of civilization. He was the god of goodness and light forever opposed to the forces of evil and darkness. He was associated with the wind and the planet Venus.

Tlaloc

His name means "He Who Makes Things Sprout." He was the god of rain and the controller of weather. As such, he was greatly feared as being able to cause floods or droughts, or to take human life by sending hurricanes or fierce lightning storms.

Aztec Gods

Gods played an important part in the lives of the Aztecs, who believed that their gods had the power over the land and sky.
Over 60 different gods were worshipped, and each god represented a different part of the natural world and everyday life.

1. Can you find out what each of these gods represented?

    Huitzilopochtli _____

    Quetzalcoatl _____

    Tlaloc _____

2. Create and design your own Aztec god. Give him/her a name and describe what he/she will represent.

    Name: _____

    Represents: _____

    _____

    _____

    _____

    _____

3. Draw and color your Aztec god on the next page.

My Aztec God

God's Name: _____

THE AZTECS

Aztec Clans

Most of the Aztec people were "commoners." Their jobs were as farmers, builders, craftsmen, or traders. Each group of commoners belonged to a clan or calpulli. Within each calpulli there were about 100 houses. One elected official called the "headman" represented the group whenever decisions had to be made. Each calpulli controlled local law and order, and provided education and emergency help for its members.

Discuss these in a group.

1. Are there similarities and differences in the way our local government is run today?

2. Is this a more effective way to run a government? Give reasons. What are the benefits?

3. Share your group's ideas with the class.

Aztec Writing

The Aztecs did not write using an alphabet. The priests and scribes wrote using a form of little pictures called "glyphs." Books were written on deer skin or the bark of the wild fig tree. Both sides of the skin or bark were written on, then folded like a map. These folding books were called codices (singular: codex).

- Draw your own codex about your life.

The Aztec Calendar

The Aztec year was divided into 13 periods of 20 days each.

1. How many days in the Aztec year? _____ days

2. Calculate the difference between our calendar year and an Aztec year. _____ days

Student Information

Aztec Entertainment and Games

The Aztecs used many musical instruments, because music played a large part in their religious festivals and services. The main instruments played were the flute, drums and rattles.

Poetry and oral literature were important parts of the Aztec culture, as these were ways in which history was recorded and passed down through the generations.

As an outdoor activity, the game of tlachtli was played. Tlachtli was similar to basketball in that it was played in a rectangular court, and the goal was to knock a hard ball through a stone hoop, high on the court wall.

Aztec crafts were varied. Craftworkers created beautiful designs on their materials, including carving, woodwork, metalwork, pottery, weaving and featherwork.

Hernán Cortés

Hernán Cortés was born into a wealthy Spanish family in 1485. In 1518, he was chosen to lead an expedition to the Yucatan Peninsula in Mexico.

From Yucatan, Cortés then sailed northward along the coast of the Gulf of Mexico and founded the first Spanish settlement in Mexico, now called Veracruz.

In 1519, Cortés marched towards Tenochtitlan, the capital of the Aztec Empire. In November 1519, Montezuma II, the ruler of the Aztec Empire, allowed Cortés to enter the city. Cortés took advantage of this and held Montezuma II hostage. He later had him stoned to death. In 1520, Cortés again attacked the city, tortured the new leader of the Aztecs, Cuauhtemoc, and then hanged him. He ordered that the city be destroyed.

Cortés returned to Spain with gold and jewels which belonged to the Aztecs.

Crafts of the Aztecs

Aztec workers learned a variety of crafts.

1. Research to find out what the following craftsmen would have made.

    (a) metalworkers

    _____

    (b) featherworker

    _____

    (c) potters

    _____

    (d) stonemasons

    _____

2. Create your own piece of Aztec jewelry. Draw your design here.

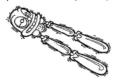

THE AZTECS

Entertainment and Games

The Aztecs worked hard, but after work they enjoyed playing or watching games such as "patolli" and "tlachtli." Many festivals were celebrated with feasts, entertainment, music and dance.

1. What musical instruments did the Aztecs play?

   _____

   _____

2. What topics can you imagine the Aztecs wrote about in their stories and poetry? Explain your reasons.

   _____

   _____

   _____

3. Describe how the game of *tlachtli* was played.

   _____

   _____

   _____

   _____

The End of the Aztec Empire

How did it happen? Was Hernán Cortés perhaps responsible for the decline of the Aztec civilization? Decide for yourself.

Compile a profile of Hernán Cortés. You will need to include: When and why did Cortés first visit the Valley of Mexico? How did Cortés take over the city of Tenochtitlan? How did he kill Montezuma II? What treasures did he take back to Spain? Did Cortés end the Aztec Empire? Explain.

_____

_____

_____

_____

_____

_____

_____

_____

Looking for more information? Try the Internet and these keywords.

Aztecs   *Tenochtitlan*   *Montezuma II*   *chocolate*   *calpulli*   *Hernán Cortés*

Student Information

Roman Republic

The Roman Republic was established in 509 B.C., after the king was overthrown. The new government elected two officials called consuls, to head the government. Consuls could only serve for a year. The senate was the most powerful government section in the Roman Republic. Senators could serve for life, they conducted foreign policy and organized government finances.

The Roman Republic lasted nearly 500 years, and because of its strong heads of state, senators and places where people could voice their opinions, this form of government was very successful.

The Roman Forum

The Roman forum was an important part of the Roman government where people could go and express their opinions. It served as the administrative and legal center of government. Romans would go to the forum to hear people speak. Residents built shops and temples around the edges of the forum, and it became the community center of Rome by the mid-100s B.C.

Roman Empire

After the Republic had been destroyed, the Roman Empire was established in 27 B.C. and lasted until A.D. 476.

The Roman emperors had the ultimate authority, but the republican institutions of government were still kept. However, the citizens' assemblies had very little power. The emperors made the laws and were the head of the army.

Mapping Activity

The map below shows the Roman Empire as it was 1,800 years ago. Many of the countries shown have a name different from what they are called today.

1. Color the Mediterranean Sea blue.

2. Use your atlas to find out the modern names of these countries.

   (a) Aegyptus _____

   (b) Britannia _____

   (c) Hispania _____

   (d) Sicilia _____

   (e) Terraconensis _____

   (f) Cyrenaica _____

   (g) Italia _____

   (h) Belgica _____

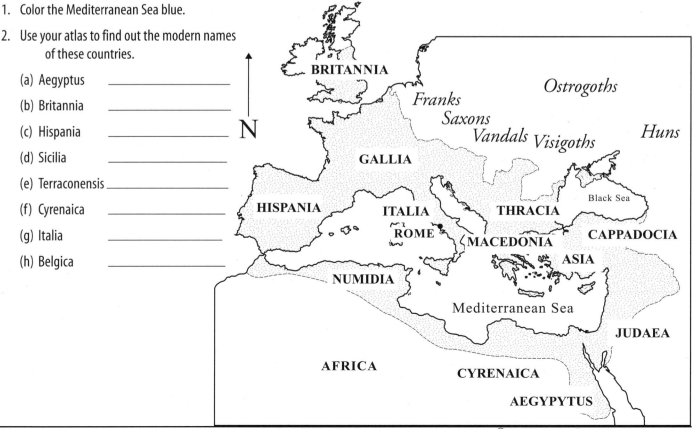

THE ROMANS

Who were the Romans?

The Roman Empire began when the tribe known as the Latins took over the city of Rome, in Italy. This tribe began to conquer all the lands around Italy. The Romans then built towns, introduced the language of Latin, and also introduced the Roman way of living to many people. About 60 million people lived in countries which made up their Empire.

Read and complete the following activities to find out more about these fascinating people.

Roman Government

When the Romans first set up their state in 509 B.C., a republic was established to govern Rome. Forums were held to discuss political issues. However, with the death of Julius Caesar in 44 B.C., powerful men were waiting to seize power over Rome, and the Roman Empire was established.

1. Describe a republic, a forum and an empire.

    Republic _____

    _____

    Forum _____

    _____

    Empire _____

    _____

Important Dates in Roman History

Over several centuries, the Romans built up a huge empire by attacking surrounding countries around the Mediterranean Sea and in Europe. The countries ruled from Rome were known as Provinces of Rome, under Roman rule.

1. Use the following information to complete the time line showing these important dates in Roman history.

    55 B.C. – *Julius Caesar's first invasion of Britain.*

    A.D. 410 – *The Roman army leaves Britain.*

    A.D. 122 – *Emperor Hadrian has a wall built across northern England to keep the Picts and Celts out of Roma territory.*

    509 B.C. – *The Etruscans are driven out of Rome and the Roman Republic is founded.*

    A.D. 79 – *Mt. Vesuvius erupts. Pompeii is destroyed.*

    197 B.C. – *Spain becomes a Roman Province.*

    753 B.C. – *According to the legend of Romulus and Remus, Rome is founded.*

    27 B.C. – *Octavianus declares peace in the Roman world, and he becomes Augustus, the first Emperor of Rome.*

    44 B.C. – *Julius Caesar is murdered.*

    A.D. 43 – *Emperor Claudius' army invades Britain.*

    146 B.C. – *New province of Africa is established.*

    A.D. 80 – *Emperor Titus opens the world's largest amphitheater, the Colosseum.*

753 B.C. – Rome is founded.

AD 410 – Roman army leaves Britain.

Student Information

Roman Baths
The wealthy Romans had baths in their own homes, but the majority of the Romans bathed at the many public baths. The bathhouses actually became meeting places for the Roman people, a form of recreation.

The Roman Emperors built these lavish public baths to encourage daily exercise and bathing. There were usually many rooms inside the bathhouses, consisting of the steamrooms, indoor pools of warm, cold and hot water, and massage rooms.

Surrounding the baths were libraries, gymnasiums and gardens, to encourage the Romans to attend.

Because the Romans did not use soap, bodies were cleaned by applying oil, and having the dirt and sweat scraped off, using a scraper called a strigil. This process was usually performed by the slaves, who worked in the bathhouses.

Roman Clothing
Romans wore simple clothes made of wool or linen.

A gown called a tunic was worn by both men and women. This garment hung to the knees or below and was often also used as nightclothes. The soldiers wore a short form of the tunic. Over the tunic, a large sheet was draped over the left shoulder. This was called a toga for the men, and a palla or stola, for the women. The stola was a longer version of the palla and hung to the floor.

White was always worn by the men, while clothing of the upper class Romans had a purple border. The women's clothing may have been dyed various colors.

Roman Housing
Wealthy Romans had large homes with many rooms. As in our homes, each room had a specific purpose.

The *atrium* was the main entrance hall or courtyard. It quite often contained a garden and fountain or pool and an opening in the roof.

The *triclinium* was the formal dining room. People ate while reclining on large couches.

The *culina* was the kitchen, where the meals were prepared before serving. Because it was used by slaves, it was usually dark, smoky and hot.

Roman Clothing

Roman people wore underclothes, as we do today. A tunic was worn over the underclothes. Roman citizens wore a toga over their tunic. Women often wore a stola.

1. Describe a tunic, a stola and a toga.

   Tunic

   _____

   _____

   Stola

   _____

   _____

   Toga

   _____

   _____

2. Color each of these pictures of Roman clothing.

THE ROMANS

Roman Town Life

Most Roman townspeople lived in crowded blocks of apartments, three to five stories high. Each apartment consisted of five or six rooms, and was set around a courtyard or garden. The wealthy Romans lived in large houses of 20 – 30 rooms. These Roman houses were built around a courtyard called an "atrium." Most rooms were small and windowless. This was for privacy and to prevent burglary. Often, shops were built at the front of the large houses.

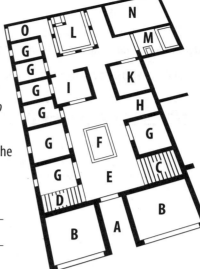

KEY

A. Entrance passage
B. Shops
C. Staircase for family
D. Staircase for servants
E. Hall
F. Rainwater basin
G. Bedrooms
H. Side rooms
I. Living room
J. Passageway
K. Small living room
L. Garden courtyard
M. Kitchen
N. Dining room
O. Back door

1. Read the passage above and use the information to decide whether the floor plan shown is that of the home of a wealthy Roman.
   Give three reasons to justify your answer.

   (a) _____

   (b) _____

   (c) _____

2. Describe these rooms. (a) Atrium _____

   (b) Triclinium _____

   (c) Culina _____

Keeping Clean

All Roman towns had a public bathhouse.

Find out the answers to the following questions.

1. What was the bathhouse used for? _____

   When? _____

2. Why were there so many rooms in the bathhouse? _____

   _____

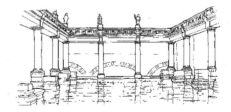

3. Who visited the baths? _____

4. What did the slaves do in the baths? _____

5. What were the oils and strigil used for? _____

Did You Know?

The Romans used money to buy things just as we do today. All coins had the Emperor's head on one side. In order of value, the main coin denominations were: dupondius, sestertius, denarius and aureus.

1. Make a list of 10 things the Romans may have bought with their coins.

   _____

   _____

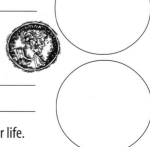

2. What designs do you think may have been on the reverse side of the coins?

   _____

   _____

3. Design both sides of a coin to represent the importance of two things in your life.

THE ROMANS

The Latin Language

Latin was the official language of the Roman world. Many of the words we use today come from Latin.

Can you find 10 or more words which we use today which have been derived from a Latin word? Explain the meaning of the Latin Root used in each word.

Word	Latin Root	Meaning

Write a paragrph using the ten words. Illustrate your paragraph.

THE ROMANS

Hadrian's Wall – A Roman Structure

1. Highlight the keywords.

When the Roman Emperor Hadrian visited Britain in A.D. 122, he ordered a stone wall to be built across the north of England to guard the northern frontier of Roman lands from the Picts and Celts of Scotland.

The wall stretched 76 miles from the east to the west coast. Every mile, a fort, or mile castle, was built. As many as 1,000 soldiers may have lived in the barracks at each fort. The walls were up to 6 meters high and 3 meters thick, and a ditch was built to make it difficult for the invaders to get to the wall to climb it. Over the years traders set up shops near the forts and towns developed.

2. Discuss in a small group.

Explain how you think Hadrian's Wall was built. Think about:
Where did the stones come from? Who constructed the wall and what materials, tools and equipment did they use? How were the ditches dug? Where did the builders of the wall live? How long would it take to complete? How would the same wall be built today—nearly 2,000 years later?

Share your ideas with other class members.

Romans – Builders and Engineers

Although the Romans were not great inventors, they were excellent engineers and builders. Many Roman-built roads, buildings and bridges have lasted over 2,000 years.

1. Write the number of the structure next to its label.

(a) *crane* ☐   (b) *circular building* ☐   (c) *arched bridge* ☐   (d) *roads* ☐

(e) *amphitheater* ☐   (f) *aqueduct* ☐   (g) *overshot waterwheel* ☐

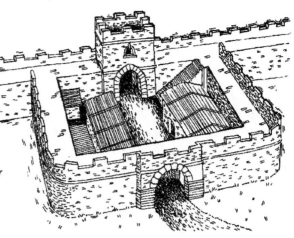

Color this mile castle.

2. Name these structures in order of which you think is the MOST important to LEAST important.

MOST IMPORTANT

_____

_____

_____

_____

_____

_____

LEAST IMPORTANT

3. Explain which of these structures built by the Romans has made the most impact on our lives.

_____

_____

_____

_____

_____

_____

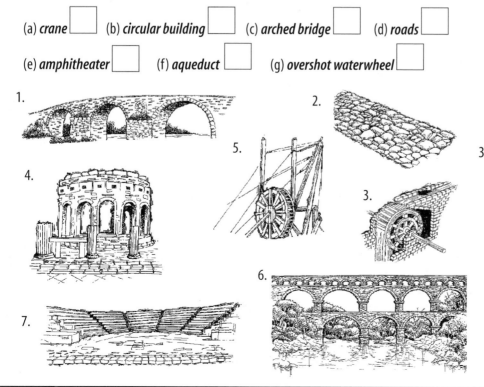

Student Information

Roman Foods

To start the day, breakfast was usually a light meal of bread and cheese. Lunch was eaten just before midday, and was usually fruit and meat or fish and perhaps some olives. Dinner was the main meal of the day and because it needed to be finished before sunset, the meal began in the late afternoon.

The meals for wealthy Romans were cooked by their house slaves in the kitchen, using pots and pans, some made from lead. The evening meal was divided into three courses. The first course was usually a taster of eggs, fish, or vegetables. Wine was served with the meal. The main course usually involved meat, fish, or poultry and cakes or fruit for dessert. Poorer Romans did not eat such lavish meals and rarely ate meat or fish—mostly breads and fruit.

Foods were cooked in ovens or on top of an open fire. Food was mostly eaten fresh, as there was no way to preserve it. Many spices were used in Roman cooking. Herbs such as coriander, fennel, mint and sage were used freely because they were easily grown. Spices were also imported from places such as India. Pepper was a favorite and nutmeg, cloves and ginger were also enjoyed. Spices and sauces were added to much of Roman cooking because it helped to disguise the taste of food that had lost its freshness.

Roman Numerals

1. What numbers do these letters represent?

    (a) I = _____   (b) X = _____   (c) V = _____   (d) L = _____

    (e) C = _____   (f) D = _____   (g) M = _____

2. Write your age in Roman numerals.

    _____

3. Write today's date in Roman Numerals.

    _____

Roman Mosaic

Wealthy Romans loved to decorate the walls, floors and ceilings of their homes with little tiles of different colored stones or bricks. These were called mosaics. Thousands of pieces were set into elaborate patterns or pictures.

1. Design a mosaic pattern of your own.

2. Draw your pattern on a sheet of paper and color it.

THE ROMANS

Roman Education

At the age of seven children learned reading, writing and arithmetic. When they were 11, the children went to secondary school to be taught by a Grammaticus. Literature, history, geometry and astronomy were studied. This Roman alphabet was used to write stories, poems, speeches and books.

1. Use this Roman alphabet to write:

    (a) Roman

    _____

    (b) alphabet

    _____

2. Research to find out how a wax tablet and a stylus were used by the Romans.

    _____

    _____

Foods and Cooking

Complete a report on Roman foods. You will need to include the following information.

1. Types of food eaten for breakfast, lunch, dinner. _____

    _____

    _____

2. How were the foods prepared? Where? By whom?_____

    _____

3. Types of herbs and spices used in cooking? Why?_____

    _____

    _____

4. How was the food cooked? Stored? _____

    _____

Roman Calendar

The Roman calendar was originally divided into 10 months, later 12 months, to make one year. Each year had 355 days. The Roman year began on March 1 but in 153 B.C. this was changed to January 1. In 46 B.C., Caesar declared the year to have 365 days in it. This was called the Julian calendar. The Romans had an eight-day week.

Can you put these Roman months in order?

Junius	*October*	*Martialis*
Januarius	*Aprilis*	*September*
Augustus	*December*	*Julius*
Maius	*November*	*Februarius*

1. _____ 2. _____ 3. _____

4. _____ 5. _____ 6. _____

7. _____ 8. _____ 9. _____

10. _____ 11. _____ 12. _____

THE ROMANS

Student Information

Roman Gods and Goddesses

The Romans worshipped several major gods, among them, Jupiter and Mars. However, many more gods were an important part of the Roman belief in the power that the gods and goddesses had over their lives.

Mars was the god of war, the son of Jupiter and Juno. Vesta was the goddess of the hearth, the hearthfire and the household. Jupiter was the ruler of all the gods and men. Minerva was the goddess of wisdom, the arts and defensive war. Janus was the god of gates, doors, beginnings and endings, represented by two faces—one looking forward and one looking backwards. Mercury was the god of commerce, skill of hands, quickness of wit, eloquence and thievery. Vulcan was the god of fire and metalworking and the husband of Venus. Saturn was the god of agriculture and the harvest and ruled during a golden age. Venus was the goddess of love and beauty. Juno was the wife of Jupiter and the queen of the gods. Also, she was the goddess of all women and marriage.

City of Rome

According to Roman legend, in 753 B.C., twin brothers Romulus and Remus established a settlement on the Palatine Hill, overlooking the Tiber River. Some legends say that Romulus and Remus were the descendants of the Greek Trojan hero, Aeneas, who founded a settlement in central Italy after the Greeks destroyed Troy. Aeneas was the son of a Trojan prince and a Greek goddess. He was the founder of the city of Lavinium.

The first known settlers of Ancient Rome were called the Latins and they lived on Palatine Hill about 1000 B.C. The Latins also inhabited many neighboring towns in the region surrounding Rome. In about 600 B.C., Etruscans took control of Rome. They had the most advanced civilization in Italy, and Rome grew from being a village, to having roads, temples and public buildings.

The City of Rome

Research Activity—Find out:

1. Who were Romulus and Remus? _____
   _____
   _____

2. Where was Palatine Hill? _____
   _____
   _____

3. Who was the Trojan hero, Aeneas? _____
   _____
   _____

4. Who were the Latins? _____
   _____
   _____

> ### Looking for more information?
> ### Try the Internet and these keywords.
>
> | | | | | |
> |---|---|---|---|---|
> | Ancient Rome | republic | forum | empire | toga | Hadrian's Wall |
> | mosaics | Roman numerals | | emperors | colosseum | Roman gods |

THE ROMANS

Roman Sports and Entertainment

1. Read the passage below. Find the correct words from the passage to fit the word spaces in the "Colosseum" word search. Highlight the keywords.

			c					
					m			
c	o	l	o	s	s	e	u	m
	m							
		p	e			p	i	
r	n		m		r			k
o								
		s			r			
					s			

Public sports and entertainment in Rome was held in amphitheaters or arenas. The most famous amphitheater is the Colosseum in Rome, built by Emperor Nero. Trained warriors called gladiators fought each other in a violent battle until one gladiator was dead.

Chariot races took place on a long oval arena called a circus. Over 200,000 people came to watch these races. Each chariot team had to complete seven laps to win the race. Romans loved to listen to music, and watch Greek and Roman dramas with colorful masks and costumes. Comedies, mimes and pantomimes were also a popular form of Roman entertainment, performed in theaters.

2. Debate the topic—**GLADIATORS ARE ENTERTAINING.**

Shops and Shopping

The shops in Roman towns were open to the streets. Shoppers went from place to place to buy the goods they needed. Streets were busy and noisy when the shops were open selling their fresh foods.

1. On a large piece of paper, draw a busy Roman street market with shops selling their breads, meats, fruits, jewelry.

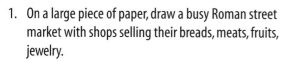

Roman Jewelry

1. Design a piece of jewelry which may have been worn by a Roman man or woman on his or her toga or tunic.

Roman Gods

Romans believed that all aspects of their lives were guided by gods and goddesses. By visiting temples to worship the gods, the Romans hoped that the gods would be pleased and bring them good fortune and health.

1. Find out the duties of the following Roman gods.

Jupiter _____

_____

Mars _____

_____

Vulcan _____

_____

Saturn _____

_____

Janus _____

_____

Venus _____

_____

Minerva _____

_____

Juno _____

_____

Mercury _____

_____

Vesta _____

_____

THE MAORIS OF POLYNESIA

Who are the Maoris?

Over 1,000 years ago a large group of people migrated south, across the Pacific Ocean in canoes to the land they called "The Land of the Long White Cloud." These people became known as the Maoris, and they settled in the islands known today as New Zealand. The Maoris established themselves in a hostile land and had to survive in a colder climate. Maori people developed their own culture and lifestyle.

Complete the following activities to find out more about the Maori people of Aotearoa (New Zealand).

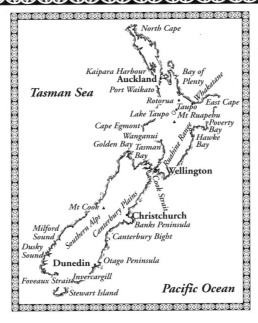

Mapping Activity

Use the map above and an atlas to answer the following questions.

1. In which hemisphere is New Zealand? _____

2. This means it is _____ of the Equator.

3. Complete the following islands, which, along with New Zealand, are some of the major island groups that form Polynesia.

   (a) C_____ Islands   (b) P_____ Island

   (c) E_____ Island   (d) S_____

   (e) T_____   (f) T_____

   (g) F_____ Islands   (h) H_____ Islands

   (i) M_____ Islands

4. What are the names of the other two divisions in the Pacific Ocean?

   _____ and _____

5. In which direction is New Zealand from the Cook Islands? _____

6. Which country is further south—Australia or New Zealand? _____

7. What is the Maori name for New Zealand? _____

8. Give four Maori place names on the North Island.

   _____   _____

   _____   _____

9. Why do you think there may be more Maori names of places on the North Island than the South Island? _____

   _____

   _____

How did the Maoris cross the Pacific Ocean?

To travel through the tropical islands in the Pacific Ocean south to New Zealand, the Maoris needed special boats. In fact, they joined two large canoes to transport people, food, animals and belongings for their long journey.

Consider and discuss the following questions. Share your ideas with the class. Write your findings.

1. What do you think the canoes were constructed from?

   _____

   _____

2. What animals would these people have taken with them on their journey?

   _____

   _____

   _____

3. Make a list of 10 things these people may have taken with them.

   _____   _____

   _____   _____

   _____   _____

   _____   _____

   _____   _____

4. Describe their feelings as land was sighted by the people.

   _____

   _____

   _____

   _____

   _____

   _____

THE MAORIS OF POLYNESIA

How did the families live?

1. Look at this picture of a Maori village and answer the following questions.

    (a) Why do you think this village is surrounded by a high wooden fence? _____

    _____

    (b) Describe the huts in the village. What materials might have been used to build these huts?

    _____

    (c) Why do you think these Maori men are sitting around the fire? _____

    _____

    What are they holding? _____

    Why? _____

    (d) How do you think the Maoris kept warm? _____

    _____

    (e) What do you think the long wooden pole in the center of the village was used for? _____

    _____

2. On a separate piece of paper draw what you think the inside of a Maori hut looked like.

Maori Village Life

1. Choose the information from the boxes to fill the spaces in this puzzle.

| *kainga* – a Maori village |
| *whare* – any sort of Maori building |
| *Tohunga* – a wise and honorable man |
| *powhiri* – a traditional welcome given by elders to ward off evil spirits; invitations |
| *marae* – central open meeting place |
| *koha* – a gift |
| *mana* – honor; power |
| *Rangatira* – the chief of the tribe |
| *tapu* – forbidden, sacred   *pa* – fortified village |
| *hapu* – family groups belonging to a tribe |
| *whanau* – several generations of one family group |
| *iwi* – a tribe of Maoris |
| *hongi* – traditional greeting of Maori people by pressing noses together |

2. Write three sentences using as many of these words as possible to show their meaning.

    _____

    _____

    _____

    _____

    _____

www.worldteacherspress.com **Ancient Civilizations**

THE MAORIS OF POLYNESIA

Student Information

Tiki

A tiki is a Maori neck pendant usually made from greenstone or jade. The tiki is in the form of a human figure. The hands have three fingers and the legs are usually bent underneath the body. The Maori call these pendants "heitiki."

Although there is a connection between the mythological figure, Tiki, who was believed to be the first man, the tiki usually takes the form of a female.

Maori Cooking

Because the Maoris did not have pots or pans to cook in, they cooked most of their food in an earth oven called a "hangi." The hangi was made by digging a shallow pit in the ground and placing hot coals and stones in the pit.

The food would be placed on the top, covered with leaves and then with earth. In this way, the food would be baked or steamed.

Kumara and taro were two root vegetables which were a basic food for the Maoris. They ate these vegetables for most of the year. Gourds are vegetables like pumpkins. The Maoris ate the vegetables, and then dried the outsides to make containers for carrying water or other objects.

Clothing

Maori clothing was all handmade using natural fibers, grasses, furs and feathers. Both men and women wore a short skirt-like garment similar to a kilt. Traditionally, Maori men never wore clothes when going into battle. Above their skirt, Maori women wore a tight-fitting bodice with geometric patterns, usually in red, black and white. Warm cloaks, often made of dog fur, were worn in colder areas.

What is a Tiki?

Answer the following questions.

1. Explain what a tiki is.

   _____

   _____

2. What is it made from?

   _____

   _____

3. How are tikis worn?

   _____

   _____

4. Who owns a tiki?

   _____

5. What do the Maoris call a tiki?

   _____

6. Draw your own tiki.

THE MAORIS OF POLYNESIA

Religion and Rituals of the Maoris

1. Read the following passages about the religious beliefs of the Maoris. Choose the correct words to complete the sentences.

learning   certain   important   believed   terrible

priests   Maoris   rituals   encouraged   life

taught   sacred   gods   properly

The _____ believed that _____

objects, places and even people were _____ or

forbidden. This was called "tapu." If someone broke a tapu the

Maoris _____ that _____ things

would happen. The Maoris had special _____ in

each tribal group. These priests played an _____

part in Maori _____ because they conducted

_____ and communicated with the

_____. The priests _____ people to

behave _____ towards others. These God

_____ _____ god. Children were

_____ about the gods when they went to their

house of _____.

What did the Maoris eat?

Below is a list of words relating to the foods the Maoris ate and how they were cooked.

1. Can you find each of them in the word search?

kumara	yams	taro
oysters	clams	bird eggs
gourds	fish	mussels
moa	hangi	pataka
raumeke	groper	snapper
berries	pigeon	nuts
seeds	fruit	

2. Can you find out how a hangi was used to cook foods?

_____

3. How is kumara eaten? _____

_____

4. What is a gourd? _____

_____

What did the Maoris wear?

1. List three differences between traditional Maori clothes and the clothes you wear.

_____

_____

_____

_____

_____

_____

2. This "King," or Rangatira, wore more elaborate clothing. Why do you think this might be?

_____

_____

_____

3. Discuss how a grass skirt could be made.

s	t	u	n	b	e	r	r	i	e	s	g
r	b	t	t	i	u	r	f	a	k	r	o
e	c	a	s	r	e	t	s	y	o	s	u
p	a	r	m	d	s	d	e	e	s	m	r
p	r	o	a	e	o	u	d	y	r	a	d
a	a	d	y	g	m	u	s	s	e	l	s
n	m	p	i	g	e	o	n	s	p	c	h
s	u	q	m	s	n	g	a	o	o	i	s
e	k	e	m	u	a	r	h	k	r	c	i
a	k	a	t	a	p	h	a	n	g	i	f

THE MAORIS OF POLYNESIA

Student Information

Maori Carvings

Using simple stone tools, Maori craftsmen created elaborate and beautiful carvings in bone, wood, or stone. Their designs were carved into jewelry, war clubs, canoes, masks, statuettes doors and house furniture.

Pakeha

New Zealand was originally inhabited by the Maoris of Polynesia, but during the 18th Century, white Europeans, known as "Pakeha," arrived. The Maoris lived a simple life, in harmony with their environment. Over the next 200 years, the Pakeha brought many things to change the culture and lifestyle of the Maoris.

Larger ships meant that travel to places further away was possible. New grains for crops, animals for food and dairy were brought from England and other European countries. Building materials and tools were more readily available to construct more permanent housing. The skills of reading and writing meant the introduction of education.

Unfortunately, the Pakeha also brought diseases previously unknown to the Maoris and this killed many of them. Freedom was also lost as the Pakeha began to claim land which had previously belonged to the Maoris. The Maoris felt that their culture would also be lost as more and more Maoris married Pakeha, and the two cultures blended to become one.

Maori Carvings

Only special Maori craftsmen had the skills to make the many beautiful wooden carvings using just basic stone tools. Many of these carvings were decorated with swirling spirals and represented sea monsters, grotesque forms and human figures.

1. Complete the other half of this elaborate wooden carving.

2. Make a list of other objects which were elaborately carved by these skilled craftsmen.

   _____

   _____

   _____

   _____

   _____

   _____

   _____

3. How were these objects used?

   _____

   _____

   _____

THE MAORIS OF POLYNESIA

Face Tattooing

Many Maori men and women carved patterns into the skin on their faces using a tiny bone chisel. This was called tattooing, or "moko." Each moko was a unique design.

Look at the example given.

1. Do you think this process would be painful?

   YES   NO

2. Are these designs symmetrical along the nose line?

   YES   NO

3. Draw a moko design of your own.

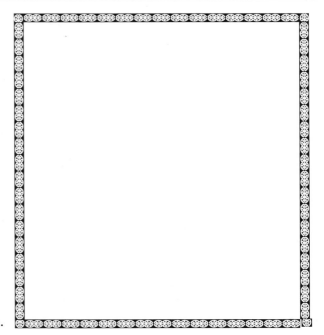

Maori Gods and Goddesses

Tangaroa	Protector of the sea and father of fishes and reptiles
Taneor	Protector of the forests
Tanemahuta Tawhiri-matea	God of storms
Rongo	God of peace and cultivated lands
Tu-matauenga	God of war
Kahukura	Another god of war whose symbol was a rainbow
Turanga	A river god
Rangi	Sky father
Tu	God of war
Tane	The giver of life, signified all people
Tinirau	A god who lived in the ocean

To the Maoris, the gods and goddesses kept their life in harmony and held power over all natural things.

1. Order this list of gods from those you think may be the most important to the least important.

   (a) _____   (b) _____

   (c) _____   (d) _____

   (e) _____   (f) _____

   (g) _____   (h) _____

   (i) _____   (j) _____

   (k) _____

2. Give the reasons for your choice.

   _____

   _____

Who or what is a Pakeha?

The Maoris had lived in harmony with their environment for many centuries. "Pakeha" is the name given to the white Europeans who arrived in New Zealand during the 18th Century. They brought with them many things from Europe which they thought would be of benefit to them in their "new" land.

1. Name three things the Pakehas brought to New Zealand.

   (a) _____

   (b) _____

   (c) _____

2. Name three things the Pakehas did which harmed the Maoris.

   (a) _____

   (b) _____

   (c) _____

3. Explain how the Pakehas almost destroyed the Maori people's culture, beliefs and spirit.

   _____

   _____

   _____

   _____

   _____

   _____

Student Information

Moa

The moa is an extinct species of flightless bird which lived on both North Island and South Island of New Zealand. Its size varied from a large turkey to a height of three meters. It ate fruit and leaves and had a small head with a long neck. The moa had small stout legs and no wings. It probably became extinct over 1,000 years ago because of the destruction of its forest habitat.

Kiwi

The kiwi is the name of a flightless bird, which lives in New Zealand. The name comes from the Maori word "kiwi-kiwi," which refers to the whistling call of the males.

The females of the species are larger than the males. Kiwis have long flexible bills with slit-like nostrils at the tip. At the base of the bill there are long hair-like feathers, which may help the bird see at night.

Kiwis have small, dark eyes and they do not see very well. To find food, they use their keen senses of smell and hearing. Their small useless wings are hidden by body feathers.

Maori Art

Spiral designs were found on most pieces of Maori art and carvings.

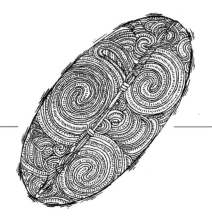

1. Use the example shown here to design a spiral art design of your own in an oval shape.

2. Join all the spiral designs together to form a class display.

THE MAORIS OF POLYNESIA

Fun and Recreation for the Maoris

Doesn't this look like fun? It was a giant swing for young and old in the center of the village.

1. Describe how it was used and how it would feel to have a swing.

_____

_____

2. Write in the correct vowels in the passage below to make this information make sense!

The M_____r___s used m___s___c and d___nc___ to ___xpr___ss their f___ ___l___ngs.
The d___nc___s were called "h___k___s." Different types of haka were p___rf___rmd for different
___cc___s___ ___ns.

An ___ggr___ss___v___ h___k___ was performed before b___ttl___. The h___k___ could be used
t___ c___l___br___t___ the h___ppy t___m___s, and m___ ___rn during s___d t___m___s.
M___ ___r___ p___ ___pl___ also had different styl___s of s___ng___ng, and they used a
v___r___ ___ty of m___s___c___l ___nstr___m___nts to pl___y their m___s___c.

Flightless Birds

The moa and kiwi are two flightless birds. One is extinct, but the other is still found in New Zealand.

Explain the difference between these two birds.

Kiwi

_____

_____

_____

_____

_____

_____

_____

_____

_____

Moa

_____

_____

_____

_____

_____

_____

_____

_____

Looking for more information? Try the Internet and these keywords.

Maoris   Polynesia   Pacific Ocean   Tiki   Kiwi   Pakeha   Moko   Moa

ABORIGINAL AUSTRALIANS

Student Information

During the Ice Age, New Guinea, mainland Australia and Tasmania were joined together, but separated from Asia by open sea. Australia's first settlers could have arrived here via two possible routes:

Route 1:   Through Sulawesi to New Guinea and then south.

Route 2:   Along the Nusatenggara island chain to Timor and then south.

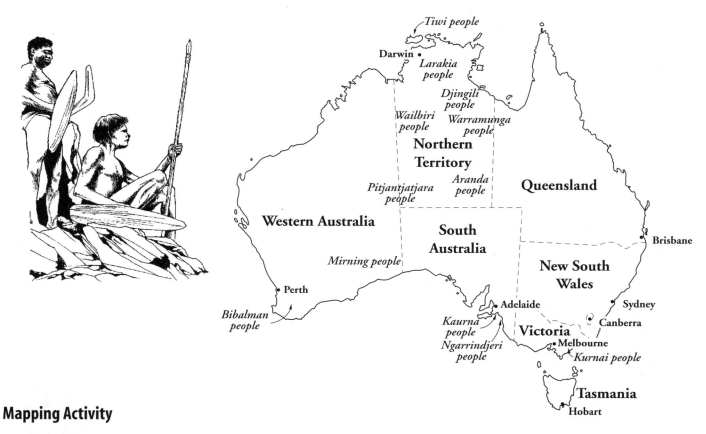

Mapping Activity

1. Use the information on the map above to complete these questions.
    In which Australian State or Territory will these Aboriginal Australian language groups be found?

    (a) Bibulman _____   (b) Kurnai _____

    (c) Aranda _____   (d) Warramunga _____

    (e) Kaurna _____   (f) Tiwi _____

    (g) Djingili _____   (h) Pitjantjatjara _____

    (i) Ngarrindjeri _____   (j) Larakia _____

    (k) Wailbri _____

ABORIGINAL AUSTRALIANS

Aboriginal Australians have been the inhabitants of the continent of Australia for over 40,000 years.

These people believe that their ancestors walked across the land, making the mountains, rivers, plants and animals as they went.

They lived in relative harmony with the land, fishing, hunting and gathering, and developed a highly organized pattern of living which varied according to the seasons and their travels.

Complete the following activities to find out more about the origins and culture of Aboriginal Australians.

Where did they come from?

The first Aboriginal Australians probably came from the countries forming what we now call Asia. Although there was less sea between Australia and these countries 40,000 years ago, the people must still have used rafts or boats to cross the ocean.

1. Use an atlas to reconstruct two different routes the people may have taken on their journey to reach Australia from Asia.

Route 1 _____

_____

_____

_____

_____

Route 2 _____

_____

_____

_____

_____

Aboriginal Groups

1. Use these words to rewrite this passage correctly.

territory *language* *larger* *300*

reluctant *tribes* *traveled* *sacred*

Australia *families* *common* *settled*

Aboriginal _____, originally formed as family groups, _____ and

then _____ in particular parts of _____. These groups of

_____ met with other groups, and intermarried and formed _____

groups known as _____ groups. This is because they shared a _____

language. It is estimated that there were over _____ of these "language"

groups throughout Australia. Each language group had its own _____ which

was its spirit-home. They were _____ to leave this area which contained many

_____ sites.

2. Draw the type of boat that you think might have been used for the journey. How would it have been made? What was it made of?

3. Describe what you think this journey would have been like: Dangers faced? Foods? Belongings? Distance covered?

_____

_____

_____

_____

_____

_____

_____

_____

ABORIGINAL AUSTRALIANS

Student Information

Aboriginal Housing

There were three basic housing varieties. One type of housing was built by using several sheets of bark, which were bent in the middle to form an inverted "V."

In the rainy season, and in the cold weather, Aborigines made more substantial shelters to keep out the rain and the cold.

Another type of shelter was an oval or circular hut built on a framework of sticks, and crisscrossed with other boughs. This was then covered with bark or branches. Some of these were made waterproof by using mud or clay.

During the wet season, huts were built on poles above the ground. Each hut was rectangular, with forked corner posts, which supported a framework of saplings, covered with bark, with the roof also made of bark. To keep the mosquitoes away, a smoky fire was built under the elevated hut.

In some areas, caves and rock shelters were used as homes. Because the Aborigines were nomadic and moved camp regularly, the houses were not built as permanent dwellings, but as temporary shelters.

Providing Fire

When the Aborigines moved camp, they usually carried fire with them in order to start a new fire when they made camp again.

Aborigines needed fire to cook their food and to keep warm at night. Fire was also used to send messages to other groups. The Aborigines often set the bush on fire to generate new growth, with the ash serving as fertilizer for new plants. Fire was needed to make new tools and weapons. The smoke and flames from the fire in the bush helped to flush animals out, when they were being hunted for food.

The firestick used the friction of two sticks being rubbed together to start a fire.

Living with the Land

Aboriginal Australians learned to adapt to the Australian landscape to survive. They did not dramatically change their environment. Instead, they appreciated the resources their environment provided, and developed special skills so they did not disturb their natural surroundings.

1. Complete the following table to find out about some of the skills used by Aboriginal Australians.

Word	skill + "ing"	Word
track		what?
fish		for?
dig		for?
cook		what?
gather		what?
dream		about?
paint		on what?
hunt		for?

ABORIGINAL AUSTRALIANS

What types of houses did Aboriginal Australians live in?

Answer the following questions about housing.

1. Why do you think this house has been built above the ground?

   _____

   _____

   _____

   _____

2. Why do you think this house has been built with a high roof?

   _____

   _____

   _____

   _____

3. What are these shelters made from? How are they held together?

   _____

   _____

   _____

   _____

4. What is this house made from? How many people might live in here?

   _____

   _____

   _____

   _____

5. Do you think Aboriginal Australians planned to live permanently in one house? Explain your answer.

   _____

   _____

   _____

   _____

   _____

Making Fire

Fire was an important "tool" which was used in a variety of ways. As well as for cooking foods, fires were used for signaling. The Aboriginal Australians also set fire to the bush vegetation to generate new growth; the ash from the fire fertilized the land.

1. Make a list of some ways Aboriginal Australians used fire.

   _____

   _____

   _____

2. Describe how smoke and fires helped Aboriginal Australians hunt for animals.

   _____

   _____

   _____

   _____

3. What is a firestick? How is it used?

   _____

   _____

   _____

4. Order the sentences below to explain the procedure used to make fire.

A	A little dried grass is placed under the sticks in the hole.
B	The soft stick is held firmly in the hole by the feet.
C	The smoldering powder is gently blown into a flame.
D	One hard and one soft stick are used.
E	The hot powder produced by the friction begins to smolder.
F	The hard stick is twirled rapidly by hand in the hole.

Step 1 _____

Step 2 _____

Step 3 _____

Step 4 _____

Step 5 _____

Step 6 _____

Student Information

Hunters

The men were the hunters and usually hunted in twos or threes. They would hunt large animals or fish to take home to the women and children in the camp. Kangaroos, emus, lizards, wallabies and snakes were all part of the food hunted by men. They used mainly spears and boomerangs to capture their prey.

Weapons

Many types of tools and weapons were used to capture their prey. One of these was the woomera, which held a spear in place so as to be able to throw it longer distances. Fish hooks were used to catch fish. Shields were carved from the trunks of trees. Axes were used to kill prey and chop trees and saplings. Lil-lil clubs were used to club animals when they were close enough. Sharp spears were used to spear and kill the animals. Fish spears were thrown at fish through the water to capture them. Boomerangs were thrown at animals to stun them long enough to be captured.

Gatherers

The women were the gatherers of nuts, yams, berries, seeds, eggs, small animals and wood for the fires. The foods were collected in pandanus baskets, or large palm fronds or leaves. A digging stick was used to extract small animals or vegetables from under the ground. A form of bread was made by crushing seeds into a flour, then adding water, and cooking in the coals of a fire.

Mostly the large animals were tossed onto the hot coals of a fire or immersed under the hot coals to be cooked. Water was collected using wooden carved bowls or large fronds from nearby palm trees.

Aboriginal family groupings

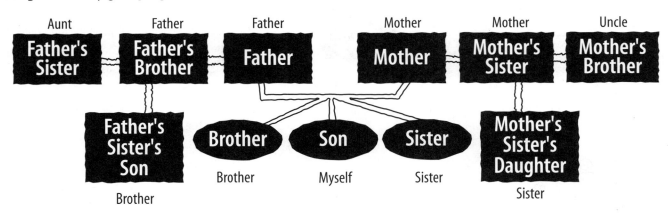

1. Explain how this family grouping is similar and different from your own family grouping.

Similar _____

_____

_____

Different _____

_____

_____

ABORIGINAL AUSTRALIANS

Hunters

The men were the hunters in Aboriginal Australian society. It was their job to provide meat for their family.

1. List six animals the men may have hunted.

_____   _____

_____   _____

_____   _____

2. Can you name the following hunting tools and weapons?

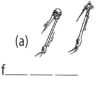

(a)

f___ ___ ___

h___ ___ ___ ___ ___

(b)

l___ ___—l___ ___ ___

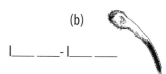

(c)

a___ ___

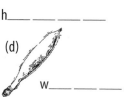

(d)

w___ ___ ___ ___ ___ ___ ___

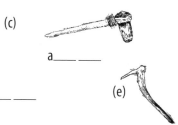

(e)

b___ ___ ___ ___ ___ ___ ___ ___

(f)

f___ ___ ___

s___ ___ ___ ___ ___ ___

(g)

s___ ___ ___ ___ ___ ___

3. Explain how one of these was used to hunt for food.

_____

_____

_____

What did the Aboriginal Australians eat?

Coastal areas provided different foods from those found in desert areas. The people ate a variety of foods which were gathered from vegetation or hunted. Foods eaten included seeds, nuts, berries, fruits and tubers. Kangaroos, fish, lizards and other animals were hunted for their meat.

1. Can you find these foods in the word search below?

ants	bandicoot	wallaby	wombat	lizard
emu	turtle	nuts	wild yams	waterlily
grass seed	bustard	acacia	fish	eggs

Gatherers

Women were traditionally the gatherers. This meant gathering the foods from nearby vegetation.

1. Make a list of six foods which the women may have gathered.

_____   _____

_____   _____

_____   _____

2. How was the food cooked?

_____

3. In what was the food collected and carried?

_____

4. What was the "digging stick" used for?

_____

5. Explain how this woman is collecting water.

_____

_____

_____

e	t	g	e	l	t	r	u	t	y
m	o	r	g	y	e	w	b	y	l
u	o	a	c	a	c	i	a	b	i
l	c	s	s	s	w	l	h	a	l
i	i	s	g	t	d	d	s	l	r
z	d	s	g	u	n	y	i	l	e
a	n	e	e	n	o	a	f	a	t
r	a	e	t	a	b	m	o	w	a
d	b	d	r	a	t	s	u	b	w

ABORIGINAL AUSTRALIANS

Music, Dancing and Ceremonies

1. Find the words in the passage to complete the puzzle correctly.

   Dancing and singing are an important part of Aboriginal Australian life.

   In dances called corroborees, the dancers imitate or mime the movement of animals or retell a story.

   Music is made by clapping boomerangs or sticks together to make a rhythmic beat.

   A wooden instrument called a didgeridoo (or didjeridu) is made from a hollow branch. Music is made by blowing into the long pipe.

   Sacred ceremonies and rituals are restricted to men only. These more elaborate ceremonies may last for days.

2. Perform a mine, with a partner, which imitates an animal's movements or tells a story.

3. Perform your mime for the class.

4. Accompany your performance with a rhythmic beat.

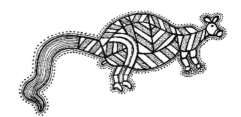

ABORIGINAL AUSTRALIANS

Aboriginal Australian Society

Read the information below and highlight the key points. Compare traditional Aboriginal Australian society to the society in which you live today by answering the questions below.

Aboriginal Australian society was very structured and complex. Each person had his or her special place within the society. There were rules and strict patterns of behavior which the people were expected to follow.

1. Write five rules of behavior you are expected to follow.

   (a) _____

   (b) _____

   (c) _____

   (d) _____

   (e) _____

Each child in the group had a special guardian who was responsible for educating that child about his or her spiritual life.

2. Describe a similar person in your life who is responsible for your wellbeing.

   _____

   _____

   _____

Children were allowed a lot of freedom to play games and experience life. Girls helped their mothers gather and prepare food, and the boys hunted with their fathers.

3. Describe any similarities or differences to your childhood.

   Similarities: _____

   _____

   Differences: _____

   _____

Can you find out?

• What is a "***midden***"? How was it used?

   _____

• Where would you find a ***billabong***? Describe it.

   _____

• Why does a ***boomerang*** return?

   _____

• How did the Aboriginal Australians use ***hand signals*** to communicate?

   _____

Share your answers with a friend.

ABORIGINAL AUSTRALIANS

Student Information

Aboriginal Art

Many Aboriginal paintings have been found in caves.

The two styles of painting are the stick-figure paintings (mimi) and the x-ray paintings of humans, animals and fish.

The colors of red, yellow, black and white were used. The colors were taken from the natural colors found in the earth and rock. These colors were then mixed with sap and water. Brushes were made from twigs, hair, feathers, or fibers. The colors were then dotted onto the bark or rock to complete the painting.

The Dreaming or Dreamtime

Aborigines believe that the great creative and spirit beings were present at the creation of time. These beings shaped the world as it is now — the sky, the ground, hills, rocks, animals. These beings will continue to live on forever. The Dreaming relates to the belief in eternity of life. These beliefs influence the Aborigines' way of life because they have respect for all things in nature and its environment.

Art and Painting

Aboriginal Australians expressed themselves through their visual art—rock paintings, paintings on wood and bark, carvings, and even painting on the human body for sacred ceremonies. The art told of the everyday experiences of the people, and also stories of the sacred life inspired by the Dreaming beliefs.

This visual art has a strong purpose — to communicate ideas to the people.

1. Describe the technique used to paint the pictures.

   _____

   _____

   _____

2. What colors were used to paint the pictures? Where did these colors come from?

   _____

   _____

   _____

3. Design a painting of your own.

ABORIGINAL AUSTRALIANS

What is "The Dreaming"?

According to Aboriginal Australian beliefs, the Dreaming is the time when the spirit-ancestors created the Earth and all things, living and natural. This included the caves, sky, hills, rivers, trees, kangaroos, snakes, rocks and fire.

• Write a report on the significance of the Dreaming beliefs to the Aboriginal Australian people. What influences did these beliefs have on the way they lived their lives?

The Aboriginal Australian people believe they belong to the land, and the land belongs to all the Aboriginal Australian people.

Each group has its special and sacred places where ceremonies were and are still held. Uluru is one of these sacred sites associated with the spirit-ancestors of the Dreaming.

1. Do we have similar beliefs in our society? Explain your answer.

_____

_____

_____

_____

Pandanus Baskets

Women used the fibers from grasses and the pandanus palm to make baskets to carry the things they gathered.

1. Describe how you think the women may have used the grasses to make the baskets.

_____

_____

_____

_____

_____

2. List 10 things the women may have carried in the baskets.

_____   _____

_____   _____

_____   _____

_____   _____

_____   _____

The Dreaming

Aboriginal Australians did not use a formal system of writing. The great stories about this time of creation, called the Dreaming, have been passed down through generations of Aboriginal Australian people. Stories were told around the campfires at night, often with a performance to make the story more dramatic and intense!

• Read a variety of Dreaming stories.

• Try — "Tiddalik," "The Rainbow Serpent," "Flying Fox Warriors," "Why the Crow Is Black."

• Prepare a story review of one of the stories you read and share your review with the class.

• Choose one of the characters in the Dreaming stories to illustrate and color.

Looking for more information? Try using the Internet and these keywords.

Aborigines   boomerang   woomera   midden   Dreamtime   Pandanus baskets

THE GREEKS

Student Information

Greek Gods and Goddesses

Apollo was the god of the sun and therefore very important to the Greeks. He was also the god of poetry, music, prophecy, healing and archery.

Athena was the goddess of wisdom, art, industries and prudent warfare.

Poseidon was the god of the sea and horses.

Hermes was the god of boundaries, roads, commerce, science and invention.

Athens

Ancient Athens was the leading cultural center of the Greek world. Its name in Greek is Athinai. It lies at the southern end of the Attica Peninsula, and is about 8 kilometers from Piraeus, Greece's largest seaport.

The Greeks built Athens around a great flat-topped rocky hill. This hill became known as the Acropolis, meaning High City.

About 530 B.C., the Athenians built a temple on the Acropolis, and dedicated it to Athena, the patron goddess of the city. It was the largest building in the city until 480 B.C., when the Persian army captured the city and destroyed most of the buildings on the Acropolis. Northwest of the Acropolis was the Agora, the marketplace of ancient Athens. There were long rows of different kinds of shops, where the people of Athens went to buy their fresh fruit, meat and vegetables.

A new political system was introduced in Athens. It was called democracy, and the reason it was different was because every qualified citizen of Athens had the chance to help run the city's government. Women, however, were not classed as qualified citizens, and therefore could not vote. Poorer classes of people were also ineligible to vote.

Mapping Activity

Use the map to complete these activities.

1. Color the Mediterranean and Aegean seas blue.

2. Name six main towns/cities in Greece.

   _____

   _____

   _____

   _____

   _____

   _____

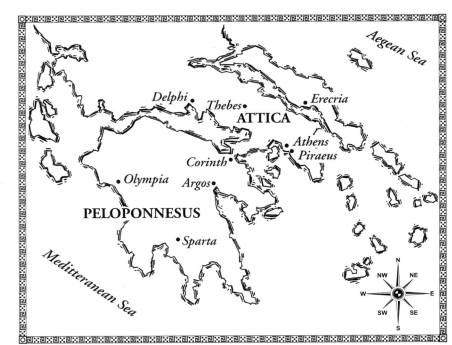

3. What is the . . .

   (a) westernmost city? _____

   (b) southernmost city? _____

THE GREEKS

Who were the Ancient Greeks?

The Ancient Greeks developed a civilization over a period of 2,000 years. The Greeks were a lively, passionate and creative people. Their greatest age of creativity was from 700 B.C. – 300 B.C. It was in this time that many ideas we still use today, such as democracy, drama and theater, history and philosophy, were developed.

To find out more about this remarkable civilization, complete the activities below.

Greek Gods and Goddesses

Greek people believed that their gods and goddesses controled all the events on Earth, and built their temples on hilltops so the gods would have the most beautiful views.

1. Find these gods and goddesses in the word search.

Poseidon
Ares
Apollo
Hera
Zeus

Hermes   Artemis
Aphrodite   Pan
Athena   Dionysos

t	a	s	a	p	n	a	p
a	s	m	p	a	r	e	h
r	k	s	h	a	r	e	s
t	l	o	r	p	a	s	u
e	e	s	o	o	n	e	e
m	p	y	d	l	e	m	z
i	i	n	i	l	h	r	o
s	o	o	t	o	t	e	n
h	s	i	e	a	a	h	y
n	o	d	i	e	s	o	p

2. Can you name what each of these gods and goddesses represents?

   (a) Athena _____   (c) Poseidon _____

   (b) Apollo _____   (d) Hermes _____

Athens – The Capital of Greece

Find out about Athens by answering the following questions:

1. Who was the city of Athens named after? _____

   _____

   _____

2. Where is Athens? _____

   _____

   _____

3. Where and what is the Acropolis? _____

4. What is the Agora and why was it important? _____

   _____

   _____

5. A system of democracy was introduced in Athens. What did this mean? Who was/was not allowed to vote?

   _____

   _____

   _____

   _____

   _____

THE GREEKS

Student Information

Clothing

Greek men and women wore a chiton, which was a belted garment made of linen or wool. The women's chiton came down to the ankles, but the men's chiton came to the knees. A full garment called a peplos, or peplum, was also worn by the Greek women. The Greeks also draped a cloak called a himation over their shoulders and arms. The usual form of footwear was sandals.

Greek Clothing

1. Find out the difference between a chiton, a himation and a peplos.

   Chiton _____

   _____

   Himation _____

   _____

   Peplos _____

   _____

2. Label and color each of these garments.

3. What did the Greek people wear on their feet?

   _____

THE GREEKS

2100 B.C. – _____

☐ – _____

☐ – _____

☐ – _____

☐ – _____

☐ – _____

☐ – _____

☐ – _____

323 B.C. – _____

Important Greek History

1. Construct your own time line, by rewriting the following important events in Greek history, in chronological order.

447–438 B.C. *The Parthenon is built.*

700 B.C. *The city-state of Athens is formed.*

2100 B.C. *The first Greek-speaking people arrive in the area now known as Greece.*

507 B.C. *Athens becomes a democracy.*

776 B.C. *First Olympic Games is held.*

323 B.C. *Alexander the Great's Empire is divided into separate kingdoms, so ending the Great Age of Greece.*

431–404 B.C. *Athens at war with Sparta. Sparta defeats Athens.*

490 B.C. *Persia attacks Greece, but is defeated at the Battle of Marathon.*

334–323 B.C. *Alexander the Great rules Greece, and defeats Persia, Syria, Egypt and Afghanistan, but dies at the age of 32.*

The Greeks at War

Each Greek city-state had an army. The men of the city fought to defend their city. Sometimes the armies fought together to ward off their enemies. The Greek soldiers were called hoplites.

1. Use this picture of a hoplite to make a list of what he wore and carried to protect himself.

Protection

_____

_____

_____

_____

_____

THE GREEKS

What did the Greeks eat?

Most Greeks ate fairly simple foods, which were cooked in olive oil over charcoal on an open fire in the kitchen.
Can you unjumble these foods and drinks of the Ancient Greeks?

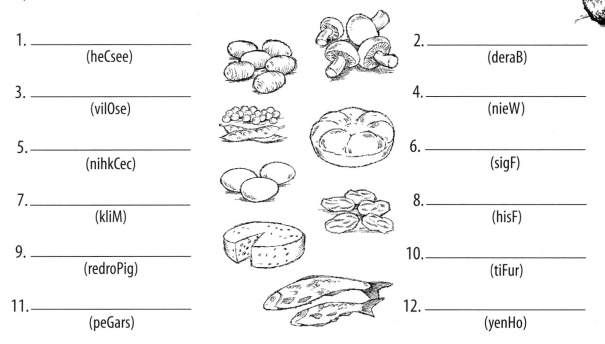

1. _____
(heCsee)

2. _____
(deraB)

3. _____
(vilOse)

4. _____
(nieW)

5. _____
(nihkCec)

6. _____
(sigF)

7. _____
(kliM)

8. _____
(hisF)

9. _____
(redroPig)

10. _____
(tiFur)

11. _____
(peGars)

12. _____
(yenHo)

Greek Words

1. Find the definition of the following Greek words.

   amphora _____

   gymnasium _____

   pentathlon _____

   amphitheater _____

   agora _____

   trireme _____

   acoustics _____

   stadium _____

   organ _____

   philosophy _____

2. Can you name this type of ship?

   _____

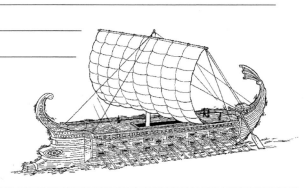

3. Put a circle around the words we still use today.

THE GREEKS

Important and Famous Greeks

1. Each of the following men contributed in some way to Greek society. Research to find out why these men are famous!

Name	Famous for ...
Hippocrates	
Socrates	
Pythagoras	
Archimedes	
Homer	
Sophocles	
Plato	
Aristotle	

Greek Sayings

1. What do the following Greek sayings really mean?

(a) Looks like a Greek god.

_____

_____

_____

(b) It's all Greek to me.

_____

_____

_____

(c) To live a Spartan life.

_____

_____

_____

THE GREEKS

Student Information

The Ancient Olympic Games

The first Olympic Games was held in 776 B.C. at Olympia in western Greece. The Olympic Games was held once every four years. For the first 13 games, only one event was held, called the stadion, which was a running race of 192 meters.

Only men were allowed to compete in the Olympic Games, and women were not even allowed to watch the competition. The men wore no clothes when they competed.

Other types of competition were added as the years progressed. In 708 B.C., the pentathlon was introduced. It comprised five disciplines — wrestling, javelin throw, discus throw, running and jumping. The prize for the winner of the event was a branch of wild olive from a sacred tree.

The Greek Alphabet

Capital letter	Small letter	Letter name	Sound
A	α	alpha	a
B	β	beta	b
Γ	γ	gamma	g
Δ	δ	delta	d
E	ε	epsilon	e
Z	ζ	zêta	z
H	η	êta	ê *or* ay
Θ	θ	thêta	th
I	ι	iota	i
K	κ	kappa	k
Λ	λ	lambda	l
M	μ	mu	m
N	ν	nu	n
Ξ	ξ	xi	x *or* ks
O	ο	omicron	o
Π	π	pi	p
P	ρ	rho	r
Σ	σ, ς	sigma	s
T	τ	tau	t
Υ	υ	upsilon	u *or* oo
Φ	φ	phi	f *or* ph
X	χ	chi	ch
Ψ	ψ	psi	ps
Ω	ω	omega	ô

The alphabet we use today was derived from the Ancient Greek alphabet. The word "alphabet" itself comes from the first two letters of the Greek alphabet —"alpha" and "beta."

1. Write your name using this alphabet.

   _____

2. How would these famous poets, playwrights and storywriters have written their names?

   Homer – poet

   _____

   Sophocles – playwright

   _____

   Euripides – playwright

   _____

   Apollonius – prose

   _____

   Sappho – poet

   _____

   Herodotus – historical prose

   _____

   Aeschylus – playwright

   _____

3. Use the Greek alphabet to write a secret message for a friend to decode.

   _____

   _____

   _____

THE GREEKS

The Ancient Olympic Games in Greece

Over 2,500 years ago, the Greeks invented the first Olympic Games.

1. Answer the questions below to find out about this wonderful sporting event.

   (a) When and where was the first Olympic Games held?

   _____

   _____

   (b) Who was allowed to compete at the Olympic Games?

   _____

   _____

   (c) What did the athletes wear?

   _____

2. Name a similarity and a difference between the Ancient and Modern Olympic Games.

   Similarity – _____

   Difference – _____

3. Which sport was the combination of five events?

   _____

   Name the events.

   _____

   _____

   _____

   _____

4. How often were the Olympic Games held?

   _____

   _____

5. What did the winners receive as their prize?

   _____

   _____

Greek Coins

From about 600 B.C. the Greeks began to use coins.

Make a list of things the Greeks may have bought using this coin. Design your own Greek coin. Don't forget to design both sides.

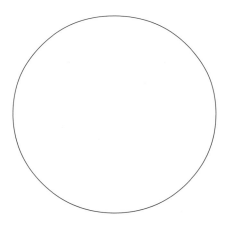

1. What did the Greeks buy?

   _____

   _____

   _____

   _____

   _____

   _____

THE GREEKS

Student Information

The Parthenon

The Greeks erected the Parthenon between 447 B.C. and 432 B.C. It is an ancient temple which overlooks the city of Athens, from the Acropolis. The Parthenon was built to honor the Greek goddess, Athena.

The Parthenon was built entirely of white marble. It is a rectangular building which measures 72 meters long , 34 meters wide and stands about 18 meters high.

A row of 46 columns surrounds the central room called the cella. The Parthenon was badly damaged when the Venetians tried to conquer Athens in 1687. The central part of the building was wrecked and most of the remaining sculpture was moved to the Acropolis Museum in Athens and the British Museum in London.

The Agora – Greek Marketplace

1. Describe what is happening in this marketplace in Athens.

_____

_____

_____

_____

_____

_____

_____

_____

_____

_____

_____

_____

_____

2. Complete the mosaic patterns around the border.

Ancient Civilizations   © World Teachers Press® www.worldteacherspress.com

THE GREEKS

Greek Pottery

Cooking pots, lamps, vases, jugs and containers were all made of pottery. Greeks decorated their pottery with patterns and scenes of everyday life in Greece.

1. Create a design of your own which shows your everyday activities.

Greek Drama and Theater

Greek theater began when the Greeks sang and danced at their wine festivals. The songs and dances became stories, then plays, which were performed in stone theatres called amphitheaters.

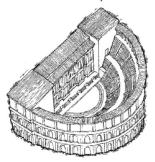

The seats of the amphitheater were sloped so that everyone looked down onto the stage. Colorful masks and costumes were worn. Some Greek plays were sad tragedies, and some were comedies.

1. Enlarge this mask design or create a full-size mask design of your own. Think about a sad or happy mask.

2. Write a short play. Use your masks in a performance of your play!

3. Compile a report on the Parthenon, which was the greatest temple in Greece. In your report you will need to include:

   (a) Where is the Parthenon located?

   (b) When was it built?

   (c) How, and why was the temple built?

   (d) Which Greek goddess was it built to honor?

   (e) Describe the temple called the Parthenon. In what condition is the Parthenon today?

Looking for more information? Try the Internet and these keywords.

| Acropolis | Athens | democracy | chiton | Olympics | Parthenon | alphabet |

Student Information

Qin Dynasty

This dynasty, or family of rulers, governed China with total domination from 221 B.C. to 206 B.C.

Shi Huang was a fierce ruler. He banned books to promote obedience, and to blot out all knowledge of the past. He ordered laborers to build new walls that connected with the older Chinese border walls to keep invaders out. This was the beginning of the Great Wall of China. The name "China" came from the name of his dynasty.

Han Dynasty

This dynasty followed the Qin dynasty, and ruled China for more than 400 years. Under the Han dynasty, arts and sciences thrived, and China became as large and powerful as the Roman Empire.

Han China expanded southwest into Tibet, and conquered North Korea and Northern Vietnam. Silk and other products flowed into the Roman Empire along the famous Silk Road.

This dynasty collapsed because of disagreements among the officials.

Ming Dynasty

The Ming dynasty ruled China from 1368 A.D. until 1644 A.D. Ming rulers restored traditional institutions such as the civil service.

Ming means "bright" in Chinese, and this period was especially important because of its arts.

Ming architects built the Imperial Palace in Beijing's Forbidden City. Artists produced porcelain, bronze and lacquerware.

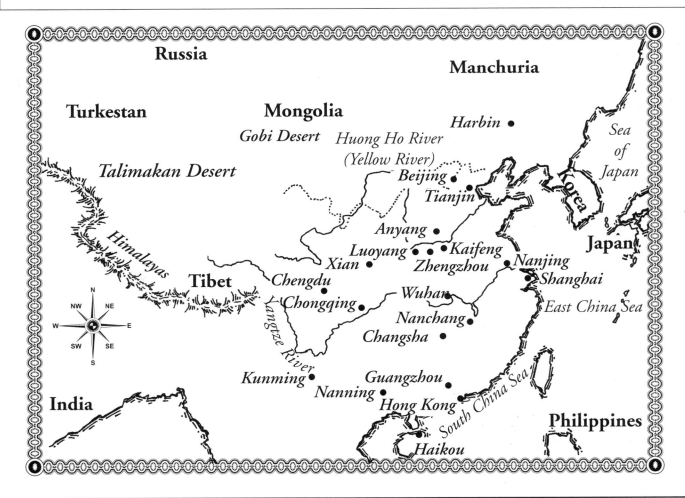

THE CHINESE

The ancient Chinese civilizations began about 8,000 years ago when people settled near the Huong Ho (Yellow) River and the Yangtze River. Vast deserts and mountain ranges meant the Chinese had little contact with the rest of the world.

By 1600 B.C., the Chinese had begun to develop their own unique culture which has flourished for over 3,500 years.

Read on and complete the following activities. Find out more about this fascinating ancient culture.

Time Line — Dynasties of China

Civilizations in China were ruled by "dynasties" for nearly 3,500 years.

Each dynasty was a sequence of powerful rulers from the same family. The first Chinese dynasty was called the Shang dynasty.

1. Unjumble the names of the following Chinese dynasties shown on the time line.

1600 B.C. – 1050 B.C.	(HGNSA)	_____
1050 B.C. – 221 B.C.	(OHZU)	_____
221 B.C. – 207 B.C.	(NQI)	_____
206 B.C. – 220 A.D.	(NHA)	_____
265 A.D. – 420 A.D.	(IJN)	_____
581 A.D. – 618 A.D.	(USI)	_____
618 A.D. – 906 A.D.	(NAGT)	_____
906 A.D. – 1270	(GSNO)	_____
1279 A.D. – 1368	(UNYA)	_____
1368 A.D. – 1644	(GIMN)	_____
1644 A.D. – 1912	(QNIG)	_____

2. Choose a partner, and prepare a short report on one of the Chinese Dynasties on the time line.

_____

_____

_____

_____

_____

_____

Mapping Activity

Use the map of Ancient China to answer the following questions.

1. Name the countries which border China.

_____

_____

_____

2. What mountain range lies west of China?

_____

3. There are three seas on the east coast of China. What are their names?

_____

_____

4. Name the two deserts to the northwest of China.

_____

5. What are the names of the two rivers along which the ancient Chinese settled?

_____

6. Name three cities/towns situated along each river.

_____

_____

7. Which city is currently the capital of China?

_____

Chinese Jewelry

Wealthy Chinese men and women wore jewelry made from gold, silver, jade, pearls and rubies.

1. Design a set of beads for a necklace.

THE CHINESE

Family Life in Ancient China

Read the information below. Form a small group to discuss the questions. Record your answers and share them with the rest of the class.

*The family was the most important unit in Chinese society.
All the generations of one family lived in the same house.*

Q. Where do your grandparents, uncles, aunts and cousins live?

_____

_____

_____

A very important household rule was that the sons and daughters should always obey their parents.

Q. Is this a sensible rule? Explain.

_____

_____

_____

_____

_____

The males in the household—fathers, grandfathers, uncles and sons—were more important than the females.

Q. Is it fair that males are more important than females? Why?

_____

_____

_____

_____

Each day, families followed a strict daily routine.

Q. What is a daily routine which occurs in your household?

_____

_____

_____

_____

_____

_____

_____

_____

Ancient Chinese families were so important that the family name, or surname, was always written first, and the given name was written last.

Q. How would you write your name in China?

_____

_____

_____

Children were taught to care for their parents in sickness and old age.

Q. How will you care for your parents? Why?

_____

_____

_____

_____

THE CHINESE

Merchant

Scholar

Artisan

Peasant

Levels of Society in Ancient China

1. Can you guess the rank, from highest to lowest, of these people in ancient Chinese society?

   1._____ 2._____

   3._____ 4._____

Read the passage below to see if you were correct!

Ancient Chinese society was divided into four classes. The scholars were in the highest class and were well respected because they could read and write.

Because the country depended on the production of food, and the peasants' work was so necessary, they were the next most important class of people. Below them were the artisans who made things that everyone needed, such as tools, cooking utensils, weapons and jewelry. The lowest class of people were the merchants. These people made nothing, but often grew wealthy from their trade of goods.

2. Write the correct order of classes in Chinese society.

   1._____ 2._____

   3._____ 4._____

3. Write one advantage and one disadvantage of being in one of these levels.

   Advantage _____

   _____

   Disadvantage _____

   _____

Chinese Inventions

Some of the world's greatest inventions originated in ancient China. The Ancient Chinese were always looking for practical ways to solve problems, and they invented many things which we still use today.

1. Match the beginnings of the names with the correct endings.

wheel	bow
ch	brella
rud	ware
fire	der
cross	barrow
com	powder
porce	work
pa	pass
mat	per
gun	ches
um	ing
lacquer	works
print	ess
clock	lain

_____   _____

_____   _____

_____   _____

_____   _____

_____   _____

_____

_____

2. Construct a model of one of these Chinese inventions.

Student Information

Chinese Writing, Printing and Paper

Paper was invented by the Chinese more than 2,000 years ago. They first used the hemp plant or the inner bark of the mulberry tree for fiber. These fibers were pounded into a pulp, flattened and dried. This paper was too coarse for writing on, and it was only used for wrapping and clothing.

The Chinese probably invented block printing. They carved characters on wooden blocks, inked the raised images and transferred the ink to paper. In about 1045, a Chinese printer named Bi Sheng made the first movable type. However, the Chinese language has thousands of different characters instead of 26 letters in an alphabet like we have. Each character is a symbol that represents a complete word.

Abacus

The abacus is a device used in China to make arithmetic calculations. It can add, subtract, multiply and divide. It is a system of rows of beads on a frame. The beads represent numbers and are strung on wires so they can be moved along the wire frame.

Foods

The Chinese had two meals a day and ate their food from small bowls using chopsticks. Chinese foods were blended with herbs and spices to create different tastes and flavors.

1. Create or find a recipe for a Chinese dinner using some of the ingredients below.

fish	ginger	snail	peanuts	yams
turnips	pork	tea	wine	grapes
yams	tofu	rice	chili	melons
beans	noodles	tangerines		

THE CHINESE

Chinese Writing, Printing and Paper

Paper was invented by the Chinese in 105 A.D.

1. Explain how paper was first made.

_____

_____

_____

_____

Between the 4th and 7th centuries the Chinese developed a printing process.

2. Describe how the printing process was developed.

_____

_____

_____

_____

The Silk Road

The "Silk Road" was the name given to the route used by Chinese merchants and traders to travel west to sell their goods in Europe. It was called the Silk Road because the traders were selling their most important export from China — silk! Traders and merchants made the dangerous and hazardous journey across the dry lands of Turkestan and Central Asia, and through Persia and Syria, to sell silks, china, bronze artifacts, jade and pottery. Camels were used to transport the heavy loads in harsh conditions.

1. Imagine! What would this journey have been like? Read more about the Silk Road and write an account of your journey along the Silk Road as a trader.

_____

_____

_____

_____

_____

_____

_____

_____

Chinese writing uses 50,000 symbols for words instead of an alphabet. It is written vertically.

3. Write a "paragraph" using only picture symbols.

Chinese numerals are older than the earliest European number systems.

4. How was the abacus used for mathematical calculations?

_____

_____

_____

_____

_____

_____

Student Information

The Silk Process

The young silkworms are put on trays. They have enormous appetites and eat continuously, night and day. The silkworms grow to 70 times their size, and shed their skin four times. When fully grown the silkworm stops eating and is ready to spin its cocoon. The silkworm spins a net made of silk to hold itself inside. The silk worker then unwinds the long delicate silk threads of the cocoon and rewinds them on to a reel. The silk is removed from the reel and twisted into skeins. Brilliant dyes may be applied to the silk yarn before it is woven. Silk yarns are woven on looms much like those used for cotton and wool. Beautiful designs and patterns can be woven on these looms.

Chinese Clothing

Generally, the more elaborate the clothing , the wealthier the Chinese person. The poorer Chinese people wore plainer materials. Women from the upper class wore more elaborate hairdos and colorful robes, and grew long fingernails. Different colors meant different messages. The color yellow was only worn by the emperor and his princes. If you wore black or blue, it meant you were an ordinary person. When you were in mourning for a dead person, you wore white.

Traditional Chinese Clothing

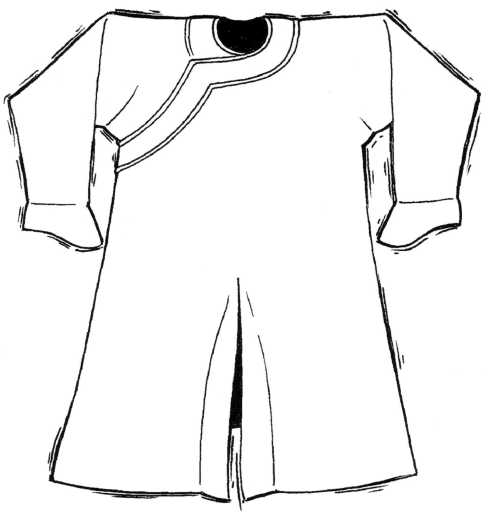

1. Name two differences between the clothing of the wealthy Chinese and that of the Chinese peasants.

2. Create a design on the Chi-Fu. Use color to highlight your design.

3. Find some more pictures of the traditional clothing of Chinese men and women. Make a class collage.

4. What did these colors indicate when worn in Ancient China?

Yellow _____

_____

Black/Blue _____

_____

White _____

_____

THE CHINESE

The Silk Process

The production of silk is one of China's oldest industries. Silkworm grubs are fed mulberry leaves and when the grubs have spun their silk cocoon, the thread is wound onto reels and spun into silk.

1. Explain the process of producing silk by describing these pictures in the correct order.

_____

_____

_____

_____

_____

_____

_____

_____

_____

_____

_____

_____

_____

_____

Feeding the silkworms

Spinning silk

Weaving the silk

Collecting mulberry leaves

Dyeing the silk

Chinese Festivals

Festival celebrations gave the Chinese people a well-earned break from their daily hard work. The Spring Festival welcomed the New Year, and lasted for several days. Families gathered to feast and watch fireworks. For the Dragonboat Festival, boats decorated with dragons' heads and tails raced on lakes and rivers.

1. Draw an image of what you think a Dragonboat Festival would have been like.

2. Make a list of special days celebrated throughout the year with your family.

_____   _____

_____   _____

_____   _____

_____   _____

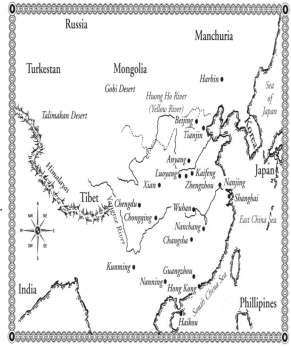

Student Information

Terracotta Army

The Terracotta Army is a collection of over 6,000 life-size terracotta statues of soldiers and horses discovered in March, 1974, at Xián. These statues were found buried in an underground tomb. The figures, all facing east, were ready for battle. They appeared to be modeled on real people because they were all individual, and accompanied by real chariots and weapons. The emperor Qin Shi Huang believed that death was just a continuation of life. Therefore, his "army" was there to protect him from his enemies, just as his "real" army had done while he was alive.

The tomb was built about 2,100 years ago for the first Qin Emperor of China. This discovery gives us clues as to how people in China may have lived over 2,000 years ago.

Religious Beliefs

In China, there were three religions, or beliefs. Each complemented the other. Read about each belief below.

Taoism
Taoists believed that people should work in harmony with nature, never against it.

Confucianism
Confucius aimed to establish loyalty to the family, good virtues and a moral society.

Buddhism
Buddhists believed that simply, happiness in life and living would be achieved by giving up luxuries.

1. In a group, discuss the benefits of each religion. Share your ideas with the class.

Taoism:_____

_____

Buddhism:_____

_____

Confucianism:_____

_____

2. Research to find out the Chinese principles of "Yin" and "Yang."

_____

_____

THE CHINESE

The Terracotta Army

Qin Shi Huang was the first Chinese emperor. He wanted to live forever. He did not, but his name lived on forever. From Qin (pronounced Chin) came the word "China."

Research to answer the questions below to find out how the terracotta army relates to the first Emperor of China.

1. Why was the Terracotta Army built?

   _____

   _____

   _____

2. Describe what was unearthed from the tomb and chambers.

   _____

   _____

   _____

   _____

   _____

   _____

3. When and where was the discovery made?

   _____

   _____

   _____

4. What is the importance of this discovery?

   _____

   _____

   _____

   _____

   _____

Looking for more information? Try the Internet and these keywords.

Silk Road	Dynasty	Inventions
Silk	yin and yang	
Terracotta Army	paper	abacus

The Great Wall of China

Read the following information about the Great Wall of China. Complete the sentences using the words below.

Dynasty   desert   Wall   Messages   built

Mongolia   smoke   mountains   Long   enemy

1. The Great _____ was also

   called the _____ Wall. It

   was _____ during the Qin

   _____ to keep out

   _____ invaders from

   _____ in the north. The wall

snaked through_____ and across _____ plains.

_____ were sent along the walls using flags,_____

and drums.

Kite Flying

It is said that the Chinese invented kites about 3,000 years ago and kite flying became a favorite pastime for the young and old.

1. Design your own kite.

THE INCAS OF PERU

Student Information

The City of Cuzco

The city of Cuzco is located in the Andes mountains in southern Peru. It was the capital city of the Incan Empire and lies about 3,400 meters above sea level. Cuzco means "navel of the earth" (center of the earth).

Incan people built Cuzco from about A.D. 1200. The Incan Empire began in 1438, and the ruler Pachacuti rebuilt Cuzco as the empire's capital. Cuzco was built in the shape of a puma. Only the Incan nobles were allowed to live in the central part of Cuzco, but about 100,000 people lived in other parts of the city. The city was protected by zigzag walls, making the entire city a fort.

In 1533, Pizarro conquered Cuzco and took over the Incan Empire, but fire swept through the city in 1536 when the Inca rebelled against the Spanish. Today, Cuzco is the trading center for local farmers. Only a fraction of the original Incan city remains — just stone foundations and ruins.

Alpacas

The alpaca is the grazing animal of South America. It is related to the camel and is usually raised for its fine wool. The alpaca can carry loads in high altitudes. Sometimes the young are killed for their meat. The Alpaca resembles the llama, and both animals are believed to have descended from the guanaco, which was a wild animal of the Andes Mountains.

Alpacas are also close relatives to the wild wool-bearing vicunas that live in the Andes.

THE INCAS OF PERU

Who were the Incas?

About 8,000 years ago, high in the Andes mountains of South America, a group of people settled in the Cuzco Valley. These people became known as the Incas. Great cities were built in the mountains and the fertile valleys were used for farming.

During the next 200 – 300 years the Incas conquered neighboring tribes in fierce battles and established their strong and powerful empire.

Up to 12 million people are thought to have lived along 4,000 km of coastline, stretching along the west coast of South America.

Complete the following activities to find out more about the powerful civilization of the Incas!

Mapping Activity

Use an atlas and the map on page 98 to complete the following activities.

1. Name the river, the mountain range and the ocean which border the Inca Empire.

_____ River

_____ Mountains

_____ Ocean

2. Name six cities/towns which were part of the Incan Empire.

_____   _____

_____   _____

_____   _____

3. Which large lake is situated close to Tiahuanaco?

_____

4. The Inca Empire once stretched along the Pacific Coast. Name the three countries which border this area today.

_____ , _____ , _____

The Great City of Cuzco

1. Write a report on this Incan city. Find the answers to the following questions to complete your report: Where was the city built? When was it built and by whom? What does the word "Cuzco" mean? Describe the layout, or plan, of this city. How was the city guarded? Who destroyed the city? What remains of the city today?

_____

_____

_____

_____

_____

_____

Animals of the Andes

1. Write three reasons why you think alpacas, llamas, vicunas and guanacos were such important animals to the Incan people living in the Andes Mountains.

(a) _____

_____

(b) _____

_____

(c) _____

THE INCAS OF PERU

Incan Society

1. The leader of the civilization of the Incas was the S ___ ___ ___

   I ___ ___ ___. The leader of the government of our country is

   called the P___ ___ ___ ___ ___ ___ ___.

2. Order the Incan society from the most
   important person to the least important.

   _____

   _____

   _____

   _____

   _____

   _____

Local Ruler

Sapa Inca

Governors of
4 quarters

Commoners

Provincial
Governor

Household
Leaders

Language of the Incas

1. Find out what the following words mean and how they relate to the Incas. (You may need to use the Internet.) Use illustrations where appropriate to support you definitions.

   adobe _____

   _____

   Quechua _____

   _____

   curare _____

   _____

   quinoa _____

   bola _____

   _____

   huaca _____

   _____

What foods were eaten?

All foods were prepared and cooked by the women. They would grind maize into flour to make breads and cakes which were cooked on hot stones.

The royal family ate more exotic and elaborate foods than the commoners.

1. Can you find all the foods eaten by the Incas in the word search?

fish	deer	honey	salt
chilli	maize	stews	herbs
llama	soups	peanuts	corn
tomato	potato	cake	avocados
beans	breads	guinea pigs	
guavas	hares		

p	s	c	h	e	r	b	s	n	r	o	c	o
e	o	i	i	e	s	d	a	e	r	b	h	t
a	d	t	h	a	r	e	s	t	h	s	i	f
n	a	m	a	i	z	e	a	o	v	a	l	s
u	c	n	b	t	s	r	a	m	a	l	l	a
t	o	y	e	n	o	h	i	a	b	t	i	v
s	v	c	a	k	e	m	s	t	e	w	s	a
y	a	n	n	c	w	v	s	o	u	p	s	u
d	f	h	s	g	i	p	a	e	n	i	u	g

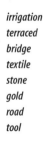

2. Underline the foods which you think were eaten by the royal family. Use these to create a meal fit for a royal Inca.

Inventions of the Incas

The Incas developed many skills, crafts and inventions.

1. Match the words on either side of the bridge to name some inventions.

irrigation	building
terraced	weaving
bridge	farming
textile	jewelry
stone	systems
gold	architecture
road	building
tool	making

The Incan Calendar

The calendar used by the Incas divided their year into 12 months of 30 days each. Each month was made up of three 10-day weeks. This left five extra days in the year which were used to celebrate Incan ceremonies. This calendar was used to decide when to plant and harvest their crops.

1. Name a similarity and a difference between the calendar we use today and the calendar of the Incas.

   Similarity: _____

   Difference: _____

2. Name three ceremonies and festivals that you celebrate in one calendar year.

   _____

   _____

   _____

Group Discussion

1. How and why did the Incas build bridges in the Andes?
2. What were the benefits of terraced farming?
3. How were the buildings built with stone? Was this successful?
4. Describe how the roads would have been constructed.
5. Why was a successful irrigation system important?
6. What necessary tools did the Incas manufacture?
7. The leader of the Incan society was often born into this position. How is the leader of our government chosen? Which system is fairer? Which is more successful to the people?

THE INCAS OF PERU

Student Information

Sapa Inca

The emperor of the Inca Empire was called the Sapa Inca. The emperor was helped by a council of noblemen who served as governors of the provinces of his empire. The Sapa Inca was responsible for looking after his people. It was his duty to expand his empire and to make sure that everyone followed the proper religious rules. All commoners paid taxes to the government by working for the government, and giving the government some of their crops. Women were required to weave a certain amount of cloth to pay their taxes. The Sapa Inca was a king and was treated well, ate good food and wore elaborate clothing.

Religion and the Incan Gods

Religion was the focus for the whole Incan Empire. Priests lived in temples and helped members of the local communities by using magic and talking to the spirits.

Gods and goddesses were said to have magical powers and each was responsible for looking after a different part of Incan life.

1. Write and illustrate a story using these Incan gods and goddesses as your main characters.

2. Design a mask to represent one of these gods.

Mamacocha mother of the sea, lakes and fish	**Pachamama** the earth goddess
Inti the sun god, kind but powerful	**Quilla** the moon god
The Stars children of sun and moon	**Illapa** god of thunder and lightning
Viracocha god of creation	

THE INCAS OF PERU

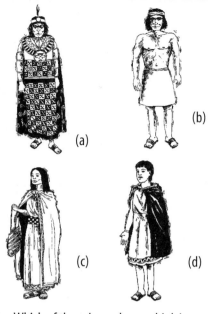

(a)

(b)

(c)

(d)

2. Which of these Incas do you think is the most important in their society? Why do you think this?

_____

_____

_____

3. How does this style of dress differ from the styles we wear today?

_____

_____

_____

_____

_____

4. Color the clothing worn by these Incas.

What did the Incas wear?

1. Read the passage below which gives you information about the clothing worn by the Incas. Choose the correct words from the box to complete the passage.

high	sash	jewelry	cloth	leather
style	cloak	colors	sandals	dresses
status	Men	decorated	worn	women

Although the basic _____ of dress did not vary, the quality of the

_____, the designs of the _____, and the colors of the

clothing _____ by the Incas, indicated their position, or _____

in society. The brighter _____, more intricate designs and highly

_____ borders on their clothing showed _____ status.

Women wore straight , sleeveless, full-length _____ which were belted

with a _____ around the waist. _____ wore short tunics with a

_____ which was knotted at the shoulders. Both men and _____

wore _____ made from _____ and fibers.

Who was the "Sapa Inca"?

All the wealth and land of the Incas was owned by the "Sapa Inca," and his every wish and command had to be obeyed.

1. Prepare a report on the life of the "Sapa Inca." Include an explanation why you would/ would not have liked to have had the position of the "Sapa Inca."

Sapa Inca – _____

_____

_____

_____

_____

_____

Time Line of Important Incan Events

1. Rearrange the information below into chronological order. Use the information to construct a time line to show important events in the history of the Incan civilization.

1532	A Spaniard called Pizarro invades the Andes Mountains and captures the last Incan Emperor, Atahuallpa
1911	Hiram Bingham finds the lost city of Machu Picchu.
1522	The Spaniards began to explore the Pacific coast of South America.
1000	The Great Incan city Machu Picchu is built in the Andes Mountains.
1536	Manco Inca's army almost recaptures Cuzco but fails.
1200	Incan civilization establishes in the Cuzco Valley.
1533	Pizarro takes a vast amount of gold from Atahuallpa, then executes him.
1438 – 1471	The 9th Incan ruler, Pachacuti, expands the Incan civilization by attacking and defeating many neighboring tribes.
1535	Collapse of the Incan Empire.

1000 _____

_____

_____

_____

_____

_____

_____

_____

1911 _____

The Home of an Inca

Use the picture to help you answer the questions.

1. What is the house roof made of?

   _____

2. What are the house walls made of? _____

3. Why do you think there are no windows in the house?

   _____

4. What do you think provides the light and heat inside the house?

   _____

5. The woman is making something—what do you think it might be?

   _____

6. What does the woman have on her head?

   _____

7. How is a pattern made in the cloth?

   _____

8. What does the woman's clothing tell you about the weather?

   _____

9. Compare this home with your own.

   _____

   _____

THE INCAS OF PERU

Craft of the Incas

Skilled craft workers made their luxury-only items for the Incan rulers and noblemen. Gold and silver were made into delicate pieces of jewelry. Pottery, decorative textiles, jeweled ornaments and wooden carvings were crafted by these skilled workers.

1. Choose two types of craft work below and create your own Incan designs.

Ary Ballus (large pot)

Jeweled dagger handle

Kero (wooden beaker)

Decorated cloth

Earplugs (earrings)

Textile tunic

The End of the Incan Civilization

1. Read the following passage and find the dictionary meanings of the highlighted words.

*In 1532, the Spanish **conquest** led by Francisco Pizarro came to South America in search of gold. They conquered the Incan Empire with only 643 horsemen and 200 foot soldiers **armed** with firearms and steel **weapons**.*

***Contagious** diseases and **infections** brought by the Spaniards also killed many of the Incan **population**.*

*The Spanish **plundered** their gold, treated the Incas poorly and forced them to work hard and change their religious ideas, which almost destroyed the **civilization** and **culture** of the Incas.*

conquest _____

armed _____

weapons _____

contagious _____

infections _____

population _____

plundered _____

civilization _____

culture _____

Inca City of Machu Picchu

The city of Machu Picchu remained a mystery until 1911, when Hiram Bingham, an American archaeologist, discovered this fabulous "lost city of the Incas." The city is built high in the mountains and is surrounded by jungle. It is about 100 km north of the Inca capital, Cuzco. About 1,000 people lived in the city.

1. Write six key facts about this "lost city." Share with a partner.

_____

_____

_____

_____

_____

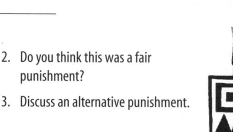

Harsh Punishments for Crime

Did you know? Incas who committed crimes were often given the death penalty. Usually offenders were pushed over a cliff!

1. Discuss how you think each of these people would have felt about this punishment.
   (a) The prisoner
   (b) The executioner
   (c) The Sapa Inca
   (d) The wife/husband of the prisoner

2. Do you think this was a fair punishment?

3. Discuss an alternative punishment.

Answers

Ancient Egypt – Page 12–13

Daily Life in Ancient Egypt

1. (a) White linen robes; shoulder-length headdress; leather sandals or bare feet; jewelry and make-up
   (b) Bread and beer was the main food and drink. Fruits and vegetables were also eaten, as well as fish, poultry, cheese and butter
   (c) Papyrus reed boats, boats with oars, then sails

Mapping Activity

1. (a) Kerma, Abu Simbel, Aswan, Esna, Luxor, Thebes, Karnak, Abydos, Akhetaten, Memphis, Bubastis, Tanis
   (b) North
   (c) Western Desert, Sahara Desert and Eastern Desert
   (d) Mediterranean Sea
   (e) Karnak, Thebes, Luxor

The Pyramids of Egypt/ Did You Know?

Teacher check

Ancient Egypt – Page 14–15

Egyptian Words

1. Alphabetical order
2. Dictionary meaning

   (a) amulet — piece of jewelry worn as a protection against evil
   (b) barter — trade by exchange of goods
   (c) embalming — to treat a dead body with preservatives
   (d) hieroglyphs — pictures (or sounds) representing an object
   (e) mummy — an embalmed or preserved body
   (f) natron — a mineral found in salt deposits used in embalming
   (g) papyrus — a kind of paper made from the stems of the papyrus reeds
   (h) Pharaoh — the title of the ancient Egyptian kings
   (i) pyramids — huge stone constructions with a square base built to hold the tombs of Ancient Egyptians
   (j) sarcophagus — a stone or marble coffin or tomb
   (k) scarabs — sacred beetles
   (l) scribe — a person making handwritten copies before the invention of printing
   (m) shaduf — a mechanism for raising water
   (n) sphinx — a stone statue with the body of a lion and the head of a man
   (o) tomb — a place for burying a corpse

3. Teacher check

The Ritual of Embalming

1. Step 1. Internal organs removed through surgical holes and stored in jars.
   Step 2. Body dried with natron then spices, oils and resins used to fill body.
   Step 3. Body wrapped in layers of linen strips.
   Step 4. Body placed in a coffin in a tomb.

2. Picture 2 – body dried with natron then spices, oils and resins used to fill body
   Picture 4 – body being placed in coffin in tomb

Ancient Egypt – Page 16–17

Famous Pharaohs

1. Teacher check

2. Teacher check

Governing Egypt

1. Government has several levels from local government levels through to the federal government.
2. (a) The "barter" system works on exchanging goods and services.
   (b) Teacher check
3. Teacher check

Papyrus for Paper

1. • Cut the papyrus.
   • Trim it into thin strips.
   • Lay it flat in layers.
   • Compact and join the layers.
   • Use the paper.

Ancient Egypt – Page 18–19

Gods and Goddesses

1. Teacher check
2. Teacher check

Rosetta Stone

1. (a) The Rosetta Stone helped to solve the riddle of the language of Ancient Egypt. Egyptian hieroglyphics were carved onto the basalt stone.
   (b) Jean-François Champollion studied the stone and deciphered the meanings of the Egyptian words.

Sphinx

1. (a) Desert near Giza
   (b) Built to protect the king
   (c) Carved
   (d) Built from limestone and cut stone blocks
   (e) Pharaoh Khafre

Hieroglyphics

1.
2. Teacher check

Ancient Egypt – Page 20–21

I Want my Mummy

1. Teacher check
2. Teacher check

Tutankhamen

1. (a) 1347 BC
   (b) 18 years of age
   (c) In the Valley of Kings
   (d) 9 years old
   (e) Howard Carter
   (f) 1922
   (g) No
   (h) Gold, jewelry, toys, trumpets, swords, arrows

(i)   The gold mask found on the mummified body
(j)   Egyptian Museum in Cairo.
(k)   Teacher check

Time for History
1. Teacher Check

The Vikings – Page 22–23

Why did the Vikings become raiders?
1. Because Scandinavia was never **invaded** by the Romans, the people and their culture thrived. The **population** increased, farmers grew crops and kept **animals** and hunted for seal and deer and **fished** the sea. However, farmland was becoming **scarce** and there was not enough **fertile** land for the growing population.

   The Vikings were experienced ship**builders** and they **sailed** in their longboats to **raid** nearby lands. They returned to their homes with their ships loaded with **treasures** and slaves. The **first** Viking raid was in A.D. 793 on the monastery on the **island** of Lindisfarne on the **east** coast of England. The Vikings slaughtered the **monks**, **destroyed** the church and **looted** its treasures.
2. Teacher check

Where did the Vikings come from?
1. Norway, Sweden, Denmark
2. Teacher check
3. Spain, France, Ireland, England, Russia, Iceland
4. Teacher check

What did the Vikings wear?
1. Teacher check

The Vikings – Page 24–25

Viking Time Line
1. 793, 795, 843, 845, 862, 866, 890, 994, 1013, 1016, 1066, 1100

Viking Invasions
1. Seville   Novgorod   Toulouse   Cordoba   London Paris
   York   Hamburg   Lindisfarne Iona   Nantes

Questions to Ponder
1.-6. Teacher check

Viking "Longships"
1. "Longships": length, ocean, inland, figurehead, shallow/sailors, shields, raiders/painted, pine, sailors/shallow
2. Teacher check

Viking Crafts and Jewelry
1. Teacher check

Viking Levels of Society
1. King, Jarls, Karls, Thralls
2. Teacher check

The Vikings – Page 26–27

Famous Vikings
1. Teacher check

Vikings at Home
1–3. Teacher check
4. a board game
5. storing food
6. valuables
7. in a cauldron
8. water

Viking Women
1. Teacher check
2. Duties – harvesting the crops; looking after the animals; children and elderly; cooking the food; spinning and weaving; looking after the land and treasures.
3. Teacher check

The Vikings – Page 28–29

Viking Words
Teacher check

Runic Alphabet
1. (a)   ship:
   (b)   raid:
   (c)   shield:
   (d)   prow:
   (e)   Sweden:
   (f)   looted:

Menu for a Viking Feast
1. Teacher check

The Native Americans – Page 30–31

Mapping Activities
1. Teacher check
2. Pacific Ocean, Atlantic Ocean, Labrador Sea, Arctic Ocean, Caribbean Sea
3. Rocky Mountains, Rio Grande River, Mississippi River, Saskatchewan River

Answers

Who were the tribes of the Great Plains?

1.
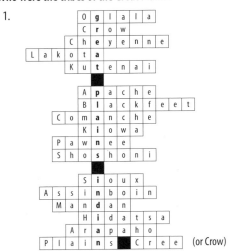
(or Crow)

Do You Know?

A vehicle without wheels used by Native Americans; two long poles harnessed at one end to a horse or dog, trailing on the ground, with a net between for carrying goods.

Native American Words

1. Missing letter is **P**.

2. *petroglyph* – a rock carving
   papoose – a Native American baby
   parfleche – a large envelope of hide used to store and carry possessions
   pemmican – dried meat pounded into a paste and made into cakes
   peace pipe – a pipe smoked by Indian tribes as a token of peace
   powwow – a ceremony accompanied by magic, feasting and dance; a meeting
   prairies – large areas of grassland with few trees

The Native Americans – Page 32–33

Erect A Tepee

1. Teacher check

What types of homes did the Native Americans live in?

1. Wooden framed buildings with cut grasses on the outside.
2. Teacher check
3. Teacher check

Nomadic Tribes

1.-4. Teacher check

How were the children educated?

1.–2. Teacher check

The Native Americans – Page 34–35

Time Line of Important Events

1. 15,000 years ago from Asia across the Bering Strait.
2. They first settled on the grassy plains of Canada before moving south.
3. They moved to the Great Plains by A.D. 850, because of the rich soil and plentiful buffalo.
4. Columbus arrived in 1492 to settle in a new land.
5.-6. The Spaniards traded guns, horses and steel knives which aided warfare and increased hunting areas.
7. The Native Americans resented the white settlers taking their land, and the white settlers forced the Native Americans to live on allocated areas called reservations.

Communication with Pictographs

Tells a story of a battle between the Indians and the Spaniards.
Answers will vary

What did the Native Americans wear?

1. Animal skins and fur
2. moccasins, buffalo hide
3. Used to protect the legs and keep warm
4. With intricate designs using flowers, beads and feathers.

The Native Americans – Page 36–37

What did the Plains Indians eat?

1.

y	t	a	e	m	d	e	i	r	d	a	s
e	w	t	u	r	n	i	p	s	i	t	a
z	h	e	s	a	i	l	a	t	t	a	o
i	s	v	e	b	c	s	n	r	p	e	e
a	u	c	s	b	o	n	t	a	e	m	t
m	n	a	o	i	d	a	l	w	m	o	w
y	f	i	o	t	o	e	a	b	m		p
p	l	u	m	s	d	b	e	e	i	a	u
e	o	t	s	b	h	c	h	r	c	f	m
f	w	n	i	d	m	i	r	r	a	f	p
a	e	l	k	r	k	r	f	i	n	u	k
h	r	t	b	e	r	r	i	e	s	b	
l	s	t	h	s	a	u	q	s	o	l	n
g	t	i	e	w	c	n	h	e	r	b	s

2. Pemmican is dried meat pounded with melted fat and pressed into cakes, then cooked.

What was the family structure of the Plains Indians?

1. 12-50 families would form a band.
2. 300 families would form a tribe.
3. – 4. Teacher check

Why were the buffalo hunted?

1.

rhia	–	hair
tame	–	meat
verli	–	liver
nudg	–	dung
tfa	–	fat
dhies	–	hides
fohos	–	hoofs
ruf	–	fur
rohns	–	horns
nebos	–	bones

2.

	f	a	**t**			
			h	i	d	e	s
	m	**e**	a	t		
			█			
		b	o	n	e	s
d	**u**	n	g			
		f	**a**	t		
h	o	o	**f**	s		
	h	**a**	i	r		
		l	i	v	e	r
h	**o**	r	n	s		

3. Teacher check

Crafts of the Plains Indians

1. – 3. Teacher check

How were the tribes governed?

The *Plains* Indian tribes *governed* their people in a democratic manner. Each band of Indians chose a *chief* to represent their people. This leader was *chosen* for his bravery, wisdom and generosity. *Important* decisions were made by the chiefs when they sat at *meetings* called tribal councils. A peace *pipe* was smoked in silence before discussions began. All men were *allowed* to voice their *opinions* before *final* decisions were made.

The Native Americans – Page 38–39

Personality Profiles

Geronimo (1834–1890) A warrior of the Chiricahua Apaches who led attacks on settlers and soldiers in Mexico in the 1870s and 1880s. His name meant "The Smart One."

Sitting Bull (1834–1909) Famous medicine man and leader of the Hunkpapa Sioux, involved in the Battle of the Little Big Horn. Went to Canada but returned to Dakota. He was a brave warrior.

Crazy Horse (1844–1877) A chief of the Oglala Sioux tribe. To seek revenge for an attack on a Cheyenne village, he led the Sioux and Cheyenne tribes in war against the American soldiers in Montana. He also led the Battle of the Little Big Horn in which General Custer and all his soldiers were killed.

Fun and Games for Plains Native Americans

1. pony racing, archery contests, hoop and ball rolling, playing field hockey, tobogganing and skating, dice rolling games, listening to stories and legends, playing lacrosse
2. Teacher check

Festivals and Ceremonies

1. The sun was important to grow their crops and provide warmth.
2. Teacher check
3. Ground to make flour; cooked; boiled with meat; dried to put in soups
4. Teacher check

Poetry

1. The words of the poem mean that the Native Americans have lost their land and find it very difficult to bear.

The Aztecs – Page 40–41

Research Activity

1. By three causeways, made of raised earth.
2. Using a grid system of canals and streets
3. Homes were made from adobe, reeds or stone.
4. Palaces, temples and pyramids were built in the center of the city.
5. Chinampas were small island gardens made by piling up mud.
6. The Great Temple; in the center of the city, used for religious ceremonies; made of limestone

Mapping Activity

1. Lake Texcoco
2. Popocatépetl
3. Gulf of Mexico
4. Teacher check

The Aztecs – Page 42–43

Order in Aztec Society

Tlatoani (King)   Cihuacoat (Deputy)   Priests and Scribes

Government Officials   Warriors and Knights   Farmers, Craftsmen

Profile of an Aztec Ruler: Montezuma II (1480 – 1520)

He was born in 1480. He was the emperor of Mexico. He ruled from 1502 – 1520. He built temples and hospitals but was disliked because of heavy taxation. He was stoned to death after the Spanish took over the city.

Time line of Important Aztec Events

1200 – Aztecs reach the valley of Mexico.
1325 – Aztecs settle on the island of Tenochtitlan.
1400 – Aztecs conquer most of the other tribes in the valley.
1500 – Aztecs become the strongest civilization in the valley.
1502 – Reign of Montezuma II begins.
1519 – Spaniard, Hernán Cortés, arrives in Mexico.
1520 – Montezuma II is killed.
1521 – Cortés destroys the Aztec Empire, Spanish rule begins.

Answers

vvvvvvvvvvvvvvvvvvvvvvvvvvvvvvvvvvvvvvvvvvvvvvvvvvvvvvvvvvvvvvvvvvvvvvv

The Aztecs – Page 44–45

What did the Aztecs wear?

1. *Similarities* – Cloak over shoulder, tie around waist
   Differences – More elaborate clothing worn by wealthy, sandals on feet, more colorful.
2. Teacher check

What did the Aztecs eat?

tomatoes, pumpkin, beans, peppers, carrots, peanuts, avocado, sweet corn, sweet potato, chili

Aztec Warriors and Wars

1. Aztec Warriors were taught when they were very *young* about fighting weapons and warfare. Only *boys* were trained to fight and it was a duty and an *honor* to fight in battle. Aztec warriors attacked neighboring tribes attempting to *steal* their crops and animals. They *captured* prisoners to use as human sacrifices to the gods. The courage, *bravery* and *strength* of these *fierce* warriors helped to *build* their Empire, and establish them as the *strongest* of all the tribes in the valley.
2. Teacher check
3. Aztec Warrior

Did You Know?

When the pod of the bean is ripe, it is dried and fermented. The cacao bean is then cleaned, roasted, hulled, blended and ground into a fine powder or made into a rich syrup.

Aztec Gods

1. Teacher check
2. *Huitzilopochtli* – the war god
   Quetzalcoatl – associated with civilization and learning
   Tlaloc – a rain and fertility god

The Aztecs – Page 46–47

Aztec Clans

1.–3. Teacher check

The Aztec Calendar

1. There are 260 days in the Aztec year
2. 105 days difference

Aztec Writing

Teacher check

The Aztecs – Page 48–49

Crafts of the Aztecs

1. (a) metalworkers – pots, swords, jewelry
   (b) featherwork – ornate decorations for clothing
   (c) potters – pots, clay bowls, cups, plates
   (d) stonemasons – huts, temples, pyramids
2. Teacher check

Entertainment and Games

1. The musical instrument the Aztecs liked to play most were the flute, drums and rattles.
2. The topics the Aztecs wrote about in their stories and poems were related to their history.

3. Tlachtli was similar to basketball in that it was played in a rectangular court, and the goal was to knock a hard ball through a stone hoop, high on the court wall.

The End of the Aztec Empire

In 1519, Cortés went to Tenochtitlan to conquer the city for jewels and gold. Cortés convinced Montezuma II to allow the Spaniards to enter the city but they attacked, and Montezuma II was taken hostage and killed. Cortés took the Aztecs' gold and jewels back to Spain.

The Romans – Page 50–51

Mapping Activity

1. Teacher check
2. (a) Egypt (b) Britain (c) Spain (d) Sicily
   (e) England (f) Libya (g) Italy (h) Belgium

Roman Government

1. *Republic* is a nation or state in which citizens elect representatives to manage their government.
   Forum is a place where business is done and courts and public assemblies are held.
   Empire is a group of nations or states under one ruler or government.

Important Dates in Roman History

1. 753 B.C.   509 B.C.   197 B.C.   146 B.C.   55 B.C.   44 B.C.   27 B.C.
   A.D. 43   A.D. 79   A.D. 80   A.D. 122   A.D. 410

The Romans – Page 52–53

Roman Clothing

1. *tunic* – a shirt or gown reaching the knees
   stola – a large robe worn by women
   toga – a looser outer garment worn by men
2. Teacher check

Roman Town Life

1. Teacher check
2. *Atrium* – is the main room of the Roman house, also served as an entrance hall.
   Triclinium – is the dining room.
   Culina – is the kitchen of a Roman home.

Keeping Clean

1. bathing and meeting place, daily
2. to include steamrooms, indoor pools, massage rooms, libraries, gyms and gardens
3. Romans who did not have baths in their homes
4. clean the people using the baths
5. to remove dirt and sweat

Did You Know?

1.–3. Teacher check

The Romans – Page 54–55

The Latin Language

Teacher check

Hadrian's Wall – A Roman Structure

1.-2. Teacher check
   Teacher check

Romans – Builders and Engineers

1. (a) 5   (b) 4   (c) 1   (d) 2   (e) 7   (f) 6   (g) 3
2.-3. Teacher check

The Romans – Page 56–57

Roman Numerals

1. (a) I = 1
   (b) X = 10
   (c) V = 5
   (d) L = 50
   (e) C = 100
   (f) D = 500
   (g) M = 1,000

2. Teacher check
3. Teacher check

Roman Mosaics

1.–2. Teacher check

Roman Education

1. (a) Roman – ROMAN
   (b) alphabet – ALPHABET

2. A thin coating of colored wax was applied to pine boards. People used the sharp end of the stylus to scratch letters into the wax. When they had finished, the curved end was used to smooth the wax so it could be used again.

Foods and Cooking

1. Breakfast was a light meal of bread and cheese. Lunch was meat, fish, olives and fruit. Dinner was the main meal, mainly meat, fish, shellfish, eggs, vegetables and sweet cakes or fruit for dessert.
2. Prepared by slaves in the kitchen using lead pots and pans.
3. coriander, fennel, mint, sage, pepper, nutmeg, ginger and cloves; to disguise the taste of food that had lost its freshness.
4. In ovens or on an open fire; eaten fresh – no storage.

Roman Calendar

1. Januarius   2. Februarius
3. Martialis   4. Aprilis
5. Maius   6. Junius
7. Julius   8. Augustus
9. September   10. October
11. November   12. December

The Romans – Page 58–59

City of Rome

1. Twin brothers; legendary founders of Rome
2. Palatine Hill is the site of Rome. It overlooks the Tiber River.
3. A Trojan warrior, he founded Lavinium near Rome
4. The first known settlers of Ancient Rome.

Roman Sports and Entertainment

1.

				c				
	R		c	o		m		
c	o	l	o	s	s	e	u	m
h	m	a	m	t	p	m	s	a
a	a	p	e	u	o	p	i	s
r	n	s	d	m	r	e	c	k
i	s		i	e	t	r		s
o			e	s		o		
t			s			r		
				s				

2. Teacher check

Roman Gods

Jupiter – god of the heavens
Mars – god of war
Vulcan – god of fire
Saturn – god of agriculture and the harvest
Janus – god of gates and doors
Venus – goddess of love and beauty
Minerva – goddess of wisdom and the arts
Juno – goddess of women and marriage
Mercury – god of commerce
Vesta – goddess of the hearthfire and the household

Shops and Shopping

Teacher check

Roman Jewelry

Teacher check

The Maoris of Polynesia– Page 60–61

Mapping Activity

1. Southern
2. South
3. (a) Cook Islands
   (b) Pitcairn Island
   (c) Easter Island
   (d) Samoa
   (e) Tonga
   (f) Tahiti
   (g) Fanning Islands
   (h) Hawaiian Islands
   (i) Marquesas Islands
4. Melanesia, Micronesia
5. Southwest
6. New Zealand
7. Aotearoa
8.-9. Teacher check

Answers

How did the Maoris cross the Pacific Ocean?

1.-4. Teacher check

How did the families live?

1.-2. Teacher check

Maori Village Life

1.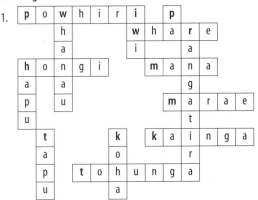

2. Teacher check

The Maoris of Polynesia– Page 62–63

Religion and Rituals of the Maoris

The *Maoris* believed that *certain* objects, places and even people were *sacred* or forbidden. This was called "tapu." If someone broke a tapu the Maoris *believed* that *terrible* things would happen. The Maoris had special *priests* in each tribal group. The priests played an *important* part in Maori *life* because they conducted *rituals* and communicated with the *gods*. The priests *encouraged* people to behave *properly* towards others. Children were *taught* about the gods when they went to their house of *learning*.

What did the Maoris eat?

1.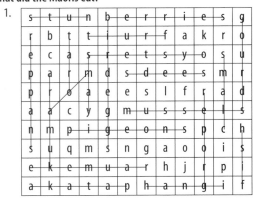

2. A hangi is an open air cooking pit, filled with hot stones. Food is added and covered with leaves.
3. Kumara is a root vegetable and can be steamed or roasted.
4. A gourd is the fruit of plants of the cucumber family. Dried shells are used for ornaments or drinking cups.

What did the Maoris wear?

1.-3. Teacher check

What is a Tiki?

1. A neck pendant worn by the Maoris
2. Greenstone or jade
3. Worn around the neck
4. Maori people
5. Heitiki

The Maoris of Polynesia– Page 64–65

Maori Carvings

1. Teacher check
2. war clubs, canoes, masks, statuettes, doors, furniture
3. As jewelry or for ceremonial or everyday use

Maori Gods and Goddesses

1.–2. Teacher check

Face Tattooing

1. Teacher check

2.-3. Teacher check

Who or what is a Pakeha?

1. education; crops and animals; tools and equipment
2. disease; claimed land; took away freedom
3. Teacher check

The Maoris of Polynesia– Page 66–67

Fun and Recreation for the Maoris

1. Answers will vary
2. The Maoris used music and dance to express their feelings. The dances were called hakas. Different types of haka were performed for different occasions. An aggressive haka was performed before battle. The haka could be used to celebrate the happy times, and mourn during sad times. Maori people also had different styles of singing and they used a variety of musical instruments to play their music.

Maori Art

1.–2. Teacher check

Flightless Birds

Kiwi – Has no tail, small useless wings, does not fly, related to the moa, long flexible bill, small dark eyes, can run swiftly, eats worms, insects and berries.

Moa – There were 13 different species, some the size of a turkey and some up to three meters tall. It could not fly, had a small head, a long neck, stout legs, no wings and ate fruit and leaves.

Aboriginal Australians– Page 68–69

Mapping Activity

1. (a) WA   (b) Vic.   (c) NT   (d) NT   (e) SA
   (f) NT   (g) NT   (h) WA/NT   (i) SA   (j) NT
   (k) NT

Where did they come from?

1.-3. Teacher check

Answers

Aboriginal Groups

1. Aboriginal *tribes*, originally formed as family groups, *traveled* and then *settled* in particular parts of *Australia*. These groups of *families* met with other groups and intermarried and formed *larger* groups known as *language* groups. This is because they shared a *common* language. It is estimated that there were over *300* of these "language" groups throughout Australia. Each language group had its own *territory* which was its spirit-home. They were *reluctant* to leave this area which contained many *sacred* sites.

Aboriginal Australians– Page 70–71

Living with the Land

1. tracking   –   animals
   fishing   –   for shellfish/fish
   digging   –   for yams/snakes etc.
   cooking   –   meat/potatoes etc.
   gathering   –   nuts/berries etc.
   dreaming   –   about the past
   painting   –   on rock/bark
   hunting   –   for kangaroo/emu etc.

What type of houses did Aboriginal Australians live in?

1.-5. Teacher check

Making Fire

1. cooking, signaling, regenerating bush, natural soil fertilizer, flushing out animals, helping to make weapons
2. The smoke and flames from fires helped to flush animals out of the bush.
3. A stick used to obtain fire by friction, either by rubbing it against another stick or by twirling it in the hands with the point in a hole in a flat piece of wood.
4. Step 1   *D*
   Step 2   *A*
   Step 3   *B*
   Step 4   *F*
   Step 5   *E*
   Step 6   *C*

Aboriginal Australians– Page 72–73

Hunters

1. fish, kangaroos, emus, lizards, wallabies, snakes, etc.
2. (a) fish hooks   (b) lil-lil   (c) axe   (d) woomera
   (e) boomerang   (f) fish spears   (g) shield
3. Teacher check

Gatherers

1. nuts, yams, berries, seeds, eggs, small animals, etc.
2. Food was cooked on the hot coals of a fire or placed beneath the hot coals.
3. wooden carved bowls; pandanus baskets; large palm fronds or leaves.
4. Used to extract small animals or vegetables from under the ground.
5. She is using a carved wooden bowl to dip water.

What did the Aboriginal Australians eat?

1.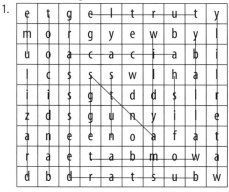

Aboriginal Family Groupings

1. Teacher check

Aboriginal Australians– Page 74–75

Music, Dancing and Ceremonies

1.

2.-4. Teacher check

Aboriginal Australian Society

1.-3. Teacher check

Can you find out?

A *midden* is a refuse heap for the rubbish from a camp site.

A *billabong* is a stagnant pool or branch of a river flowing away from the main stream.

A *boomerang* returns because of its shape, and the way it is thrown.

Hand gestures or *finger signals* were used if Aboriginal Australians met people who did not understand their language.

Aboriginal Australians– Page 76–77

Art and Painting

1. The techniques used were to paint using brushes made from twigs or fibers with colors in a dotted pattern.
2. The colors used were red, yellow, black and white — found in earth and rock.
3. Teacher check

What is the Dreaming?

1. Teacher check

Answers

Pandanus Baskets
1.-2. Teacher check

The Greeks– Page 78–79

Mapping Activity
1.-2. Teacher check
   3. (a) Olympia   (b) Sparta

Greek Gods and Goddesses
1.

t	a	s	a	p	n	a	p
a	s	m	p	a	r	e	h
r	k	s	h	a	r	e	s
t	l	o	r	p	a	s	u
e	e	s	o	o	n	e	e
m	p	y	d	i	e	m	z
i	i	n	i	l	h	r	o
s	o	o	t	o	t	e	n
h	s	i	e	a	a	h	y
n	o	d	i	e	s	o	p

  2. (a) Athena   – wisdom, art, industries, prudent warfare
     (b) Apollo   – sun
     (c) Poseidon – sea, horses
     (d) Hermes   – boundaries, roads, commerce, science, invention

Athens – The capital of Greece
1. Named after the goddess Athena, the patron goddess of the city.
2. At the southern end of the Attica Peninsula
3. The Acropolis is the great flat-topped rocky hill overlooking Athens.
4. The Agora was the marketplace of ancient Athens where the people bought fresh fruit, meat and vegetables.
5. The system of democracy allowed qualified citizens to have a direct say in running the city's government. Women and poorer class citizens were not eligible to vote.

The Greeks– Page 80–81

Greek Clothing
1. Chiton   – belted garment often of linen or wool.
    Himation   – a draped cloak over the shoulders.
    Peplos (Peplum) – a shawl worn by women.
2. Teacher check
3. sandals

Important Greek History
   2100 B.C.   776 B.C.   700 B.C.   507 B.C.   490 B.C.   447–438 B.C.   431–404 B.C. 334–323 B.C.   323 B.C.

The Greeks at War
1. Teacher check

The Greeks– Page 82–83

What did the Greeks eat?
1. cheese 2. bread 3. olives 4. wine
5. chicken 6. figs 7. milk 8. fish
9. porridge 10. fruit 11. grapes 12. honey

Greek Words
1. *amphora* – a two-handled earthenware jar to store grain or oil, pointed at the bottom.
   gymnasium – a place where athletic exercises were practiced in Ancient Greece.
   pentathlon – an athletic contest consisting of five events.
   amphitheater – a circular or oval building with rows of tiered seats around a central, open space.
   agora – a marketplace in a Greek city.
   trireme – a warship with three rows of oars on either side, banked one above the other.
   acoustics – the structural features of an auditorium hall or room that determine how well sounds can be heard in it.
   stadium – Greek running track for foot races with tiers of seats along the sides and one end.
   organ – a musical instrument made from pipes of different lengths.
   philosophy – study of truth or principles of all real knowledge.
2. trireme
3. philosophy, stadium, organ, acoustics, pentathlon, gymnasium, amphitheater

Important and Famous Greeks
  Hippocrates – the father of medicine, represented all that was good in medicine.
  Socrates – devoted his life to seeking truth and goodness.
  Pythagoras – philosopher and mathematician.
  Archimedes – mathematician and inventor, laws of levers, buoyancy, calculus, catapult.
  Homer – poet who composed the "Iliad" and the "Odyssey", about events during the Trojan War.
  Sophocles – wrote over 120 tragic plays.
  Plato – educator and philosopher.
  Aristotle – philosopher, educator and scientist.

Greek Sayings
1. (a) A beautiful, perfect-looking person.
   (b) It makes no sense whatsoever.
   (c) To live a very simple and basic existence.
2. trireme

Answers

The Greeks– Page 84–85

The Greek Alphabet
1. Teacher check

2. *Homer* – Ηομερ
   Sophocles – Σοπηογλες
   Euripides – Ευριπεδες
   Apollonius – Απολλονιυς
   Sappho – Σαπφο
   Herodotus – Ηεροδοτυς
   Aeschylus – Ησκλυς

3. Teacher check

The Ancient Olympic Games
1. (a) First games held in 776 B.C. at Olympia in western Greece.
   (b) Only men were allowed to compete.
   (c) The athletes competed nude.
2. Teacher check
3. The pentathlon was a combination of jumping, running, discus throw, javelin throw and wrestling.
4. The games were held every four years.
5. Winner received a branch of wild olive from a sacred tree.

Greek Coins
1. Teacher check

The Greeks– Page 86–87

The Agora – Greek Marketplace
1. Teacher check
2. Teacher check

Greek Pottery
1. Teacher check

Greek Drama and Theater
2. Teacher check
3. Parthenon – A temple on the hill called the Acropolis overlooking the city of Athens. Built between 447 B.C. and 432 B.C. Dedicated to Athena. Built of white marble, a rectangular building surrounded by a row of 46 columns. Only the ruins of the building remain today.

The Chinese– Page 88–89

Time Line — Dynasties of China
1. Shang, Zhou, Qin, Han, Jin, Sui, Tang, Song, Yuan, Ming, Qing
2. Teacher check

Mapping Activity
1. India, Tibet, Turkestan, Russia, Manchuria, Korea
2. Himalayas
3. Sea of Japan, East China Sea, South China Sea,
4. Talimakan and Gobi
5. Huang Ho and Yangtze Rivers
6. Nanjing, Wuhan, Chongqing, Huang Ho, Kaifena, Zhengzhou, Luoyang
7. Beijing

Chinese Jewelry
1. Teacher check

The Chinese– Page 90–91

Family Life in Ancient China
Teacher check

Levels of Society in Ancient China
1. Teacher check
2. Scholar, Peasant, Artisan, Merchant
3. Teacher check

Chinese Inventions
1. wheelbarrow   rudder
   gunpowder   compass
   crossbow   porcelain
   paper   umbrella
   fireworks   matches
   clockwork   lacquerware
   printing   chess

The Chinese– Page 92–93

Foods
1. Teacher check

Chinese Writing, Printing and Paper
1. The paper was made from fibers of the hemp plant or inner bark of the mulberry tree. These were pounded into a pulp, flattened and dried.
2. At first printing was done by carving entire pages into blocks of wood — upside down and back to front. These blocks were inked and paper pressed over them to create an image. Later, separate characters on blocks were used. These could be used over and over again.
3. Teacher check
4. The abacus consists of moveable beads on a frame. The beads represent numbers that can be used to add, subtract, multiply and divide.

The Silk Road
1. Teacher check

The Chinese– Page 94–95

Traditional Chinese Clothing
1. Teacher check
2. Teacher check
5. Yellow   – only worn by the emperor and princes.
   Black/Blue   – worn by ordinary people.
   White   – worn when mourning the deceased.

The Silk Process
1. When the eggs hatch, the grubs are fed mulberry leaves and they grow at a rapid rate. When fully grown the silkworm stops eating and spins itself a cocoon of silk on a twig. The silk workers spin the long threads of silk onto reels. Dyes are applied to the yarn before it is woven. Silk yarns are woven on looms like those for cotton and wool.

Chinese Festivals
1-2. Teacher check

The Chinese– Page 96–97

Religious Beliefs

1. Teacher check
2. *Yin –*   An element in Chinese philosophy representing the (female) qualities of darkness and cold.

   Yang –   An element in Chinese philosophy representing the (male) qualities of light and heat.

The Terracotta Army

1. The Terracotta Army was built to protect the Emperor Qin.
2. More than 6,000 life-size terracotta statues of the soldiers and horses accompanied by real chariots and weapons.
3. The discovery was made in 1974 near Xi'an.
4. It gives clues to how people in China lived 2,000 years ago.

The Great Wall of China

The Great **Wall** was also called the **Long** Wall. It was **built** during the Qin **Dynasty** to keep out **enemy** invaders from **Mongolia** in the north. The wall snaked through **mountains** and across **desert** plains. **Messages** were sent along the walls using flags, **smoke** and drums.

Kite Flying

1. Teacher check

The Incas of Peru– Page 98–99

Mapping Activity

1. Amazon River, Andes Mountains, Pacific Ocean
2. Lima, Machu Picchu, Nazca, Quito, Tiahuanaco, Cuzco, Chanchan, Moche or Santiago
3. Lake Titicaca
4. Chile, Peru, Bolivia

The Great City of Cuzco

The city is in the Andes Mountains in southern Peru. Built from about 1200 and rebuilt in 1438 under the rule of Pachacuti. Cuzco means "navel," meaning the city's role as the Empire's capital. The city is built in the shape of a puma and was guarded by huge stone walls. The Spanish explorer Francisco Pizarro conquered Cuzco 1533 and took over the Inca Empire destroying much of the city. Only foundations and ruins remain from the original city. Today, Cuzco is a trading center for local farmers.

Animals of the Andes

1. (a)   Used as beasts of burden
   (b)   For their wool
   (c)   For their meat

The Incas of Peru– Page 100–101

Incan Society

1. Sapa Inca, President
2. Sapa Inca, Governor of 4 quarters, Provincial Governor, Local Ruler, Household Leader, Commoners

Language of the Incas

1. *adobe*   –   a brick made of sun-dried clay
   Quechua   –   the language of the Incas
   curare   –   a poisonous extract from South American plants used on arrow tips to paralyze the muscles of animals
   quinoa   –   a plant grown for its grain—used to make bread, soups and beverages
   bola   –   a weapon consisting of stone or metal balls tied at the ends of a long cord
   huaca   –   a tomb, temple, or a pyramid of stone which is the dwelling place of the spirits

What foods were eaten?

1.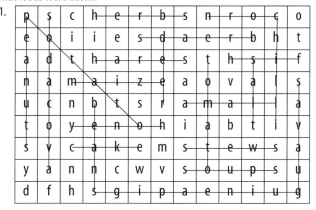

2. Teacher check

Inventions of the Incas

Irrigation systems, terraced farming, bridge building, textile weaving, stone architecture, tool making, gold jewelry, road making

The Incan Calendar

Teacher check

Group Discussion

Teacher check

The Incas of Peru– Page 102–103

Religion and the Incan Gods

1.–2.   Teacher check

What did the Incas wear?

1. Although the basic **style** of dress did not vary, the quality of the **cloth**, the designs of the **jewelry** and the colors of the clothing **worn** by the Incas indicated their position, or **status** in society. The brighter **colors**, more intricate designs and highly **decorated** borders on their clothing showed **high** status. Women wore straight, sleeveless, full-length **dresses** which were belted with a **sash** around the waist. **Men** wore short tunics with a **cloak** which was knotted at the shoulders. Both men and **women** wore **sandals** made from **leather** and fibers.

2.–4.   Teacher check

Who was the "Sapa Inca"?

1. Teacher check

The Incas of Peru– Page 104

Time Line of Important Incan Events

1. 1000, 1200, 1438 – 1471, 1522, 1532, 1533, 1535, 1536, 1911

The Home of an Inca

1. thatch (grass, reeds)
2. stones

3. for insulation
4. a fire
5. weaving cloth
6. a traditional Incan hat
7. using different color yarn
8. it is cool to cold
9. Teacher check

The Incas of Peru– Page 104

Craft of the Incas
1. Teacher check

The End of the Incan Civilization

1. conquest — the act of conquering.
    armed — equipped with or supported by arms or armor.
    weapons — an object or instrument used in fighting.
    contagious — capable of being passed on by a diseased person.
    infections — invasion of the body by micro-organisms.
    population — all the persons inhabiting a certain place.
    plundered — to steal goods and sacred items.
    civilization — a human society which has a complex cultural, political and legal system.
    culture — the total of inherited value, beliefs and knowledge.

Incan City of Machu Picchu
Teacher check

Harsh Punishments and Crimes
1.-3. Teacher check